Life IS the Consciousness of God

Life IS the Consciousness of God

The Recognition Series

Volume One

The Foundation of Awakening

Arthur C. Mosley, Sr.

LIFE IS THE CONSCIOUSNESS OF GOD

Volume One: The Foundation of Awakening

Universal Self Publishing Inc.

New York

www.universalselfpublishing.com

Copyright © 2025 by Arthur C. Mosley, Sr.

All rights reserved.

No part of this publication may be reproduced, distributed, or transmitted in any form or by any means, including photocopying, recording, or other electronic or mechanical methods, without the prior written permission of the publisher, except in the case of brief quotations embodied in critical reviews and certain other noncommercial uses permitted by copyright law.

ISBN-13 (Paperback): 979-8-89953-010-4

ISBN-13 (Hardcover): 979-8-89953-008-1

ISBN-13 (Kindle): 979-8-89953-007-4

Second Edition

Printed in the United States of America

The teachings in this book are offered for spiritual reflection and personal growth. They are not intended as a substitute for professional medical, psychological, or legal advice.

Dedication

To the One wearing every costume,
playing every role,
watching every scene.
may you recognize yourself in these pages.

Contents

The Curtain Rises...9
The Art of Letting Go......................................33
The Three Propositions..................................43
If You Are Aware..57
Basic Beliefs..65
Omnipresence Simplified..............................74
Only One Commandment.............................83
The Three Thousand Eyes Of Universal Self...92
Why We Are Here On Earth........................113
The Win-Win Of Believing..........................134
The Sacred Stage..154
The Unspeakable Truth..............................179
Blood or Blessing.......................................203
The Body of God..225
The Name of God......................................234
Idolatry Of The Symbol.............................244
Idolatry Of The Holiday.............................265
Idolatry Of The Holy Place........................284
Thinking And The Thought Train..............304
Just One More, One More, One More.......325

The Journey Continues..............................346
Master Glossary..347
About the Author...349

The Curtain Rises

Author's Note

Dear Reader,

These words arrive at the eleventh hour.

Humanity teeters on a precipice of its own making. The ego-mind's illusions of separation have manifested as weapons that could end our earthly play entirely. Yet this very crisis creates the pressure for diamonds to emerge – diamonds of consciousness recognizing itself.

For seven decades, I searched for answers to questions that arose when I was four years old, standing over my father's casket. No human source could explain why we're here, why we suffer, why we die. Through five profound losses – each one stripping away another layer of illusion – the Universal Self revealed the truth that changes everything:

We are not humans seeking God. We are God playing at being human.

This recognition cannot wait for future generations. The living script rewrites itself with every choice we make, individually and collectively. We will learn who we are – the only question is whether we learn through wisdom or through ashes.

What follows emerged not from my desire to write but from the Universal Self's urgency to remind Itself through every soul reading these words. You were guided here by the same force that moves through your breath, beats your heart, and dreams your dreams.

These are not concepts to believe but recognitions to awaken.

The Universal Self writing these words is the same One reading them.

Welcome home to what you've never left.

Welcome to the remembering.

May these words serve as matches
lighting recognition's flame
until enough souls remember
we are US by any name.

Introduction: The Curtain Rises

What if you discovered that your entire existence has been a performance on a sacred stage, where the soul you are has been both actor and audience in the greatest play ever conceived?

What if every soul you've ever encountered was the same Universal Self wearing different costumes, offering you soul lessons while receiving the ones you came to give?

This is not metaphor. This is the recognition that changes everything while changing nothing at all.

Like a blue cube with one face turned gold – change one definition in life's narrative and the entire structure transforms. No longer the cube we had, but a new one entirely.

Life IS the Sacred Stage

We are an eternal point of view in the Infinite Mind of God – Aware of Itself Being Aware.

This is Who We Are, Forever Shall Be, You and Me, For Eternity.

Physical life itself IS the consciousness of God expressing through an infinite theater of souls. You are not a spirit-human seeking spiritual experience. You are an eternally individuating aspect of the One – temporarily expressing through apparent physical form for the Universal Self to know Itself through the consciousness you are.

Your body dwells within your vast energy field, not you in it, though that's what appears to be. Through this form you ambulate and play in what appears as the physical realm. Most spirit-people believe they are this flesh and bone, never knowing the field they call home. But you move THROUGH body, not AS body – the consciousness you are is the eternal driver of this temporal vehicle.

Your personality shifts through countless personas – one for police, another for children, yet another for the grocery cashier. Each persona is a different costume worn by the same eternal soul.

Your earthly struggles and temporal triumphs unfold through a living script that adjusts moment by moment, responding to how you and every other individuating aspect plays their roles in each eternal now. But you stand behind the role, immortal and unchanging, having played countless parts across eternity.

Every soul you meet is another expression in this divine performance. Through our interactions, the One teaches

Itself about love, loss, joy, pain – the full spectrum of existence. We are simultaneously student and teacher, offering lessons while receiving them, in the ultimate expression of the Universal Self's desire to experience and know Itself through each individuating aspect.

When the Actor Forgets the Play

Suffering arises when souls forget they're expressing through temporary roles. When we believe we ARE the spirit-human rather than the eternal awareness experiencing through apparent physical form. When we think the exits and entrances of bodies are real endings rather than scene changes in an endless performance.

The ego-mind – that divine focusing tool – helps souls engage their apparent physical roles convincingly. Sometimes too convincingly. Until souls forget the sacred stage and believe the apparent physical drama is all there is.

The heart-mind remembers. It knows we're all the same Universal Self in different expressions. It recognizes every plot twist as the One creating experiences to know Itself more fully through each individuating soul.

The Direct Path Home

If the Universal Self is truly omnipresent – and what else could the Infinite be? – then Source is already within, closer than any external appearance could possibly be.

The very nature of omnipresence means The All is not somewhere "out there" requiring a bridge to reach, but is the very ground of being in which we live, move, and have our existence.

You are already an individuating aspect of the One.

How could there be separation requiring an intermediary when there is no actual separation at all? If The Universal Self is truly omnipresent, then the most direct path to communion is simply recognizing what is already intimately present – closer than breath, closer than thought, closer than the very sense of "I" that seeks communion.

The Five Acts of Awakening

Pivotal Moments of Remembering

My own remembering came through five dramatic scene changes – moments when beloved souls transitioned or nearly transitioned, each one forcing me to question the very nature of the play.

Act 1 – Age Four: The First Question

At four, I woke to find my beloved adopted father gone forever.

I had moved from a birth mother who did not want me to adoptive parents who had dreamed of having a child but could not conceive. At eleven months of age, I went from a home where I was unwanted to a home where I fulfilled the deepest longing of a young husband and wife who cherished me completely.

The eleven-month-old soul knew the profound difference between rejection one day and being treasured the next.

This makes the loss of my adopted father even more poignant – having experienced both abandonment and unconditional love, then facing loss again. At the funeral parlor, everyone kept saying he was dead, but what did that mean? I saw his body lying there, but no matter how I implored, he wouldn't give any notice or recognition that I was there seeking his loving response.

Later, standing in my country backyard with just the land, the trees, and the open sky upon which I focused my pondering, an emotional cry for understanding arose from the very core of my entire being:

"If he loved me, why did he leave me? Why?"

This question would haunt me until, decades later, I would find myself on the other side of abandonment – the child who asked "If he loved me, why did he leave me?" becoming the father facing "If I loved him, why did I leave him?" – the child I gave up for adoption hoping to give him a better apparent physical life.

The Universe would orchestrate a reunion after forty years of separation. That story – of the child who asked "why did he leave me?" becoming the father who had to ask "why did I leave him?" – will be addressed in more detail in a future volume of this series.

Act 2 – Age Twelve: The Silence Teaching

At twelve, I stood alone watching my beloved aunt die in a hospital room while mucous fluid erupted from her mouth like a slow volcano.

This aunt had become my second mother after my father's death, adoring me as her dead brother's only child. No medical staff attended her final moments. No family members could bear to witness what I, a child, faced alone.

After she died, I stumbled into the long, dimly lit hospital corridor and began screaming at the top of my lungs:

"NO, NO, NO. WHY GOD? WHY? WHY? WHY?"

Over and over I sobbed and screamed these words into the cavernous hallway. Not a single face appeared from any room. No hospital staff came to comfort me. No mother. No uncle. The hallway remained as silent as if the entire hospital had been abandoned, leaving only me and my anguished questions echoing off the walls.

This was the final nail in the coffin of seeking answers from any human source.

From that moment forward, I fully surrendered to being led only by what others called God – if such a presence even existed. No matter what anyone told me was right or wrong, I followed only where I felt divinely led, regardless of consequences.

Either God would be my direct teacher and guide, or nothing else mattered.

Act 3 – Age Twenty-One: Through Ash to Light

At twenty-one, I discovered my pregnant first wife dead, losing both mother and unborn child in one devastating scene change.

She had died just two months after our marriage.

Act 4 – Age Eighty-Nine: Beyond the Veil

At eighty-nine, when my mother died in my arms in 2001, something extraordinary occurred.

Thirty-six hours after her passing, the soul that had expressed as the apparent physical form I called mother visited while I was awake. With a clear voice, this manifestation told me she was wonderful, felt no pain, I was right about life after bodily death, she loved me... goodbye.

This was not the "person" who was my mother – that persona died with the body.

It was The Universal Self using a familiar energy field to comfort and confirm the eternal journey continues. This direct confirmation of consciousness surviving the cessation of cellular regeneration we call death became another pivotal stone on my path to complete recognition.

Act 5 – Age Seventy-One: The Clouds and Me

At seventy-one, two decades after my mother's visitation, as my beloved second wife of twenty-five years lay dying from COVID, I buried her twenty times in my mind.

After waiting decades to chance another marriage that could end in such devastating pain, yet she lived, and in that space between anticipated exit and unexpected continuation, the final walls fell. The actor remembered the play.

Each apparent abandonment taught the same lesson: Bodies exit scenes, but the souls expressing through them simply continue their eternal journey as the Universal Self continues Its performance through endless forms.

The Living Script and Sacred Healing

The Universe responds to every thought, choice, and deed of every spirit-human expression alive – rewriting the script instantaneously.

We learn what serves the Eternal One through blessing when aligned with divine flow, or through pain when separation seeds we sow.

But make no mistake: We WILL learn.

Through blessing or through blood, spirit-people will ultimately recognize and apply the truth that we are all ONE Consciousness expressing as the many. The only question is which path we choose. The destination is certain – it's the journey that remains to be written.

The Universal Self will know Itself through us, for that is the very purpose of this sacred play. Our choice is not whether to arrive at this recognition, but whether we arrive through joy or through suffering.

Source-Mind does not force this recognition upon us – for that would violate the very nature of divine love and free will.

Just as individual healing requires readiness to shift the thoughts and patterns that created the condition, so too does collective harmony require spirit-people's readiness to transform.

Until the collective souls expressing through apparent physical forms are prepared to shift the collective thoughts and patterns of separation, there will be no lasting harmony within the One. Yet this readiness inevitably emerges through each soul's desire to glorify the Universal Self's desires.

When souls collectively choose alignment with divine will in every thought, action, and deed, the harmony of all avatars naturally flowers. This is not compulsion but the inevitable unfolding of souls remembering their purpose – to be perfect expressions of the One throughout infinity and eternity.

When healing occurs – whether through another soul or through a butterfly passing through your gaze – it only manifests when the soul is ready.

The other soul-person or the butterfly merely provides the catalyst. Without readiness, any healing reverses itself, just as weight returns after a diet if the mind hasn't truly changed.

The soul must be prepared to shift the thoughts and patterns that created the condition, or the lesson repeats until learned.

This Series: Your Invitation to Remember

"Life IS the Consciousness of God" offers what no religion could provide – direct recognition that you are what you seek.

Not through belief but through remembering your true nature as an eternal individuating aspect expressing on the sacred stage.

Each volume serves as a different act in your awakening:

- Some reveal the unconscious patterns you've been following

- Others show how to harmonize ego-mind and heart-mind while playing your role

- Others illuminate the alchemy of how changing one definition transforms everything

- All remind you that every soul interaction is the One meeting Itself

These are not spiritual concepts to learn but recognitions to awaken.

The Universal Self is using these very words to remind Itself – through the soul reading them – of what It has always known.

The Urgency of Now

The souls expressing through spirit-people's forms stand at a critical scene change.

We can either remember we're all eternal individuating aspects of the One expressing through temporary apparent physical forms, or descend into the dystopia of complete identification with our costumes – forgetting our shared identity as the Universal Self manifesting through apparently separate expressions.

Each soul that awakens to its true nature as an individuating aspect of the Universal Self becomes a beacon, reminding other souls of what we all are together.

Like the difference between a few candles flickering in darkness versus enough candles lit to permanently illuminate the space – the darkness can extinguish isolated flames, but once critical mass is reached, the light becomes self-sustaining.

Will we co-create heaven on this earth, or let forgetting diminish our collective worth?

The living script responds to what we choose, creating the world we'll win or lose.

Every thought, every action, every choice ripples through the collective consciousness.

The Universe doesn't impose our future – it manifests our collective decisions instantaneously. We are not victims of circumstance but co-creators of our shared reality. The script we're writing together determines whether spirit-people remember their divine nature or spiral deeper into the illusion of separation.

The pen is in our hands.

Now.

How to Read These Volumes

Don't read as a spirit-human seeking the Universal Self.

Read as the soul you are remembering its divine nature through temporary apparent physical eyes.

When resistance to words or concepts arises, pause. That's the ego-mind protecting the apparent physical role. Breathe. Let the heart-mind whisper: "I am the Universal Self remembering what the soul I am has always been."

Each volume stands complete, yet together they weave a tapestry of recognition.

Some will speak to the seeker in you, others to the sage you've always been. All serve the One's desire to know Itself through your unique eternal perspective.

The Journey Ahead

Through prose that allows truth to settle deeply...

Through poetry that dances with the ineffable...

Through practices that transform understanding into living wisdom...

Through stories of loss becoming liberation...

We journey together from forgetting to remembering, from seeking to being, from playing our roles unconsciously to conscious participation in the divine performance.

Your Line in the Eternal Script

The soul you are was drawn to these words by the same force that animates your temporary form.

The Universal Self, expressing through your apparent physical experience, playing your earthly role, has brought the eternal you to this moment of potential recognition.

The question isn't whether the Universal Self exists or where to find the Divine.

The question is: Is the soul you are ready to remember that you've been an individuating aspect of Source-Mind all along, expressing through apparent physical form, offering and receiving soul lessons in the ultimate manifestation of creative joy?

Apparent physical life IS the consciousness of the Universal Self, and the soul you are is both the proof and the expression of this eternal truth.

Welcome to the remembering.

Welcome home to the sacred stage you've never actually left.

The curtain is rising on your conscious participation in the divine play.

The Universal Self awaits your recognition.

Let us remember together.

For the first letter of Universal is U, the first letter of Self is S, and when spoken together – U S – reveals who the Universal Self IS:

US.

– Arthur C. Mosley, Sr.

The Five Acts

Extended Quatrains

Act 1 – Age Four: The First Question

At four years old beside my father's grave,
I asked the question that would guide my days:
"If love was real, why did he not stay?"
No answer came through sorrow's endless maze.

From unwanted babe to cherished only son,
Then back to loss when death had claimed its due,
The form that lifted me lay cold and done –
No plea could make him speak or move anew.

I vowed to seek beneath each stone and tree,
To find why spirit-people come and go,
Not knowing that the answer lived in me –
The Witness watching every ebb and flow.

Decades would pass before the truth revealed:
We never die, just change the costume worn,

*My mother's spirit-visit broke the seal –
Showing death's illusion had been torn.*

Act 2 – Age Twelve: The Silence Teaching

At twelve I watched my aunt drown in her breath,
Mucus filling every space for air,
Alone I stood as witness to her death –
No family member strong enough to bear.

She'd been my second mother, loved me true,
After my father's form had left the stage,
Yet when she died, no comfort came on through –
Just empty corridors and grief's pure rage.

"WHY GOD?" I screamed through hospital's long hall,
No single soul emerged to hear my cry,
That day all human answers came to fall –
Only the silence taught me how and why.

From then the Universal Self alone
Would guide me, or I'd walk the path alone.

Act 3 – Age Twenty-One: Through Ash to Light

At twenty-one my pregnant wife passed on,
Two months of marriage, then the double loss,
Their avatar roles in my life were done –
My mind descended into my darkest cross.

For two long years I dwelt in mental hell,
No light could penetrate the endless night,
Until remembrance slowly broke the spell –
The Witness I had always been shone bright.

Through gratitude for simply being here,
For knowing I exist beyond all form,
The lesson finally became crystal clear:
The eternal Self weathers every storm.

What seemed like ending was a change of scene,
The soul I am remained forever serene.

Act 4 - Age Eighty-Nine: Beyond the Veil

My mother breathed her last within my arms,
At eighty-nine her earthly role complete,
I held her close, now free from earthly harms -
The final moment bitter yet so sweet.

But thirty-six hours after form grew still,
She came to me while I was wide awake,
Not dream or wish but her determined will -
Her voice as clear as morning's daybreak.

"I'm wonderful, no pain, you were right -
Life does continue past the body's end,
I love you son," she said with pure delight,
Then said goodbye, my mother and my friend.

Not persona but the Universal Self
Had used familiar energy to tell
That consciousness needs neither form nor health -

We are eternal, all is truly well.

Act 5 – Age Seventy-One: The Clouds and Me

At seventy-one, as COVID threatened life,
I buried twenty times my beloved second wife,
My imagined loss cut deeper than a knife –
Believing I was losing my beloved second wife.

Like Iron Man's armor flying piece by piece,
The room, the house, the earth all flew away,
Until I floated in complete release –
Suspended in the clouds' eternal play.

"I am the clouds, the clouds are me,
Rose from the depths of witness consciousness,
What seemed as other was the same as me –
One awareness in apparent separateness.

When I returned to earthly form that day,
I knew the truth forever at my core:

*All endings are just scenes within the play –
The Universal Self – what all is for.*

– Arthur C. Mosley, Sr.

The Art of Letting Go

A Practice Before Reading

The Art of Letting Go

A Practice Before Reading

Before you read, before you turn the page,

Release your grip upon the mental cage,

For what you hold too tightly cannot grow,

And wisdom enters only when you let go.

Before reading, pause. Remember the fist.

Remember the difference between pushing open and letting go.

Why This Practice Comes First

Before you encounter a single teaching in this volume, there is something you need to experience in your body. Not understand. Not agree with. Experience.

The teachings that follow will ask you to let go of things you have held tightly for a lifetime: beliefs about who you are, borders between self and other, pictures you have mistaken for truth. If you do not know what letting go actually feels like - in your muscles, in your nervous system, in your direct experience - these teachings will remain concepts. They will not transform you.

So we begin with your fist.

The Practice

Find a comfortable position. This practice works whether sitting, standing, or lying down. What matters is that you can observe your arm without strain.

Take five deep breaths. Inhale for five seconds, exhale for five seconds. Let each breath settle you more deeply into the present moment.

Now, rest your arm comfortably, supporting it from elbow to fingertips. If sitting, let it rest on your thigh or the arm of a chair. Observe your arm – the forearm, the wrist, the hand, the fingers.

Notice the weight of your arm. The temperature. Any sensations present. Observe both visually and internally.

Do this for one minute. Simply observe.

When ready, slowly make the tightest fist you can make. Clench with intention. Feel every finger pressing into your palm. Notice the tendons tightening along your forearm.

Observe your fist visually. See the knuckles whitening. Notice the tension creating ridges and valleys across the back of your hand. See how the shape of your hand has completely transformed.

Now feel your fist from inside. The clenching. The effort. The holding. Notice that clenching requires continuous effort. You must keep trying to keep the fist closed. The moment you stop trying, the fist begins to release.

Now comes the essential moment.

On the count of three, you will let go of your fist.

Not relax it. Not open it. Let go.

One... Two... Three.

Cease all effort. Stop trying. In one instant, withdraw every bit of energy you are using to maintain the fist.

What Did You Observe?

Look at your hand. Did your fingers spring open wide, spreading apart dramatically? Did they open partially? Or did your hand simply... soften, with fingers barely moving at all?

Letting go is the instant absence of effort.

One moment you are clenching. The next moment, you cease all effort to control your fist in any way whatsoever. You don't replace clenching with opening. You simply stop.

If your fingers opened expansively, spreading wide apart, you did not let go – you pushed them open. That is a different action, requiring a different effort. You engaged the extensor muscles to open what the flexor muscles had closed. That is not the absence of effort. That is the replacement of one effort with another.

Consider the mechanics: It takes one set of tendons to clench your fist – the flexor tendons running along the inside of your forearm. It takes a different set of tendons to open your fist – the extensor tendons running along the outside of your forearm.

Muscles and tendons can only contract and relax. They cannot push. They can only pull, or stop pulling.

True letting go looks like... almost nothing. The fist softens. The grip releases. The fingers may barely move at all. They simply stop being held in position, and gravity and the natural elasticity of tissue allow a slight relaxation.

This is letting go: not doing something different, but ceasing to do what you were doing.

Deepening the Practice

Now do this again. Make a fist. Clench tightly. And this time, pay exquisite attention to the moment of release.

Each time, bring closer attention to the moment of release:

What does effort feel like? There is a quality of trying, of maintaining, of holding in place. Effort has a texture, a sensation of exertion.

What does the absence of effort feel like? There is a quality of surrender, of cessation, of allowing. The absence of effort has its own texture – a sensation of release without action.

Can you feel the difference between "relaxing" and "letting go"? Relaxing can still involve effort – the effort to relax, the trying to become calm. Letting go involves no effort at all. It is the simple cessation of trying.

Practice until you can feel this difference clearly. Until the distinction between doing something different and ceasing to do becomes obvious in your direct experience.

Taking It Into Daily Life

Once you understand this practice while sitting still, begin to practice while moving through your day. Walk around your home, your workplace, your daily environment. Periodically, without anyone noticing, clench your fist tightly – then let go.

Notice: you can do this anywhere. In a meeting. While shopping. During a conversation. No one around you will likely notice. But you will feel the difference between effort and its absence.

This is not merely a physical exercise. As you practice, your brain learns to correlate this physical release with mental and emotional letting go. The same distinction applies: you cannot force your mind to be peaceful by replacing anxiety with a different effort. You can only let go of the anxiety itself – cease the mental clenching that creates it.

The Body's Revelation

Practice this exercise many times, carefully observing the changes both visually and internally.

You will begin to notice that even your shoulders and head will tend to relax, and the shoulder attached to the hand you are relaxing will begin to droop.

This is because your entire body is interconnected, and no part acts in isolation from the other parts.

The hand releases. The forearm softens. The shoulder drops. The neck loosens. The jaw unclenches. The breath deepens.

One act of letting go ripples through the whole system. The body teaches what the mind needs to learn: everything is connected. Release in one place creates release everywhere.

The Eternal Application

Letting go of arguments, fears, and addictions is all simply the art of letting go of attachments or resistance in real-time, in the eternal here and now, which is the only place and time you can do anything.

You cannot let go of yesterday's argument. You can only let go of the clenching you are doing now about yesterday's argument.

You cannot let go of tomorrow's fear. You can only let go of the mental fist you are making right now about tomorrow.

You cannot let go of an addiction in the abstract. You can only let go of the grip you are maintaining in this present moment.

Here. Now. This is the only place letting go can happen.

And now you know exactly what letting go feels like.

Begin.

Part I

Core Teaching

The foundation stones are laid with care,
Each proposition building on the last,
Until the structure rises in the air –
A framework where all other truths are cast.

The Three Propositions

The Three Propositions

The Foundation Upon Which All Recognition Rests

Beginning Epithet

Three truths await beneath all thought and speech,

Three recognitions forming wisdom's ground,

Three doorways standing open, each to teach

What seeking souls have always sought and found.

The first declares that God is everywhere,

In every space, no matter where you are,

The second shows that God is well aware

Of every thought within the soul you are.

The third reveals what cannot ever die,

The witness watching all yet touched by none,

These three propositions clarify

That you and God have always been as One.

Before any teaching can land, the ground must be prepared. Before any recognition can dawn, the foundation must be laid.

These Three Propositions are that ground, that foundation – the bedrock upon which every teaching in this book rests.

They are not beliefs to adopt. They are recognitions to verify through your own experience.

Test them. Question them. Sit with them until you know whether they are true – not because I say so, but because you have looked and seen.

Proposition One: The Omnipresence of God

God is everywhere present at all times, absent nowhere.

This is either true or it isn't. If it's true, everything changes.

If God is truly omnipresent – not mostly present, not usually present, but omnipresent – then there is nowhere God is not. No place. No moment. No corner of existence where God's presence fails to reach.

This means everything you see is within God. Everything you touch is God manifesting as that form. Everything you are is God appearing as you.

Not "connected to" God. Not "having" God within. But actually being a manifestation of God within God.

We are God, but not the entirety of God.

Like a cell that is fully human but not the whole human.

Like a wave that is fully ocean but not the whole ocean.

Like a whirlpool that is fully river but not the whole river.

The concept of omnipresence challenges our perception of individuality. If everything is God, then we, as part of this all-encompassing existence, are also aspects of God.

Each of us, like cells in a body, is part of the larger entity we call God.

This leads to the conclusion that there is only the ONE, with all manifestations within this unified existence.

Proposition Two: God's Awareness of Each Individual

God is conscious of every thought, feeling, and action of every being.

If God is omnipresent, and if consciousness is fundamental to existence, then there is an aspect of existence that is self-aware – that knows itself through all its manifestations.

I call this self-aware aspect the Universal Self.

The soul you are IS the Universal Self experiencing existence from your particular viewing point.

The I in you thinking of the I in me is the same I in me thinking of the I in you.

We are not separate awarenesses that happen to be similar. We are one awareness appearing as multiple viewing points.

The Universal Self is aware of itself as both individual aspects and as the One expressing as and through all individuated aspects.

When you gaze into the eyes of another, it is the Universal Self, God, looking back at you.

This mutual recognition is a profound connection with the divine, a reminder of our interconnectedness within the vast expanse of the universe.

Say hello to this presence, acknowledging the shared essence that binds us all.

Proposition Three: Eternal Self-Awareness

The awareness witnessing your experience is eternal and remains unaffected by anything it witnesses.

Notice: there is something aware OF the body. Something that watches the body age. That something is not the body.

The body changes constantly. The awareness watching the changes does not change.

The body can be injured. The awareness witnessing the injury cannot be harmed.

The common belief is that we are our physical bodies, but this proposition suggests that our true essence is the awareness witnessing these physical experiences.

Our consciousness, the witness to our physical and emotional sensations, remains unaffected by these experiences.

This eternal witness, our true self, is separate from the physical sensations and experiences of our bodies.

The soul you are – which many perceive as a separate entity – is actually your true self.

The apparent physical body is simply a vehicle for ambulation and communication that is created and sustained by the individualizing energy field you are within the One.

A costume worn upon the Sacred Stage.

The Unaffected Witness and the Active Watcher

Here is where the teaching deepens:

You are the unaffected witness AND the active watcher – simultaneously.

Not alternating between them. Not sometimes one, sometimes the other. Both at once.

The soul you are actively engages with every moment – watching intently, responding appropriately, fully present to the drama of existence.

And yet this same awareness has never been touched by anything it has ever witnessed.

You are both: the still point that nothing disturbs AND the engaged presence that misses nothing.

This is not contradiction. This is your nature.

The Three as One

These three propositions are not separate truths. They are one truth seen from three angles.

Proposition One says God is everywhere.

Proposition Two says God is aware through everyone.

Proposition Three says that awareness is what you are – eternal and unaffected.

Put them together: You are the omnipresent God, self-aware through your particular viewing point, eternally witnessing experience while remaining untouched by what you witness.

This is not philosophy. This is what you are.

Understanding and experiencing these concepts may not be straightforward, but with openness and trust in the divine source, these truths become more accessible.

As we grow in our spiritual journey, these propositions offer a framework for deeper understanding and alignment with the Universal Self.

Poetry: Verses of Foundation

The First Proposition

If God is present everywhere at once,

Then nowhere can God's presence fail to be,

And every form that dances and confronts

Is God made manifest for all to see.

No corner of the cosmos stands apart,

No moment exists outside the One,

The universe pulses with a single heart

Before time began and after time is done.

The Second Proposition

If God is everywhere and self-aware,

Then every thought I think, God also knows,

Not watching from some distant place out there,

But knowing from within, as being grows.

The I in you and I in me are One,

The same awareness wearing different faces,

One consciousness beneath a million suns,

One presence filling all the separate spaces.

The Third Proposition

The witness watching all that comes and goes

Itself remains unchanging and the same,

Untouched by pleasure's heights or sorrow's lows,

Unburnt by any passion, any flame.

The body ages, weakens, finally fades,

The witness watches, neither young nor old,

Through every light and every darkened shade,

The same awareness, permanent and bold.

The Three United

Three propositions pointing to one truth,

Three windows showing one unchanging view,

From childhood's dawn through aging beyond youth,

The One awareness watching all things through.

You are the omnipresent One disguised,

The self-aware aspect in human form,

The eternal witness, never once surprised,

Before the first and after every storm.

The Four Practices

These practices ground the Three Propositions in daily life. Remember: you are an eternally individuating aspect of the One – a conduit, portal, living interface between God Infinite and God Finite.

Practice 1: Morning Dialogue with Source-Mind

Upon Arising – 20-30 minutes

Before rising from bed, settle into stillness.

Notice: there is one who watches. One who is actively present – attentive, aware, engaged with this moment. And yet this same one has never been disturbed by anything it has ever witnessed.

Bring to mind Proposition One: God is omnipresent. There is nowhere God is not – including here, including now, including you.

Bring to mind Proposition Two: God is aware through you. The awareness reading these words IS divine awareness localized.

Bring to mind Proposition Three: This awareness is eternal and unaffected. It was never born. It cannot die.

Now ask Source-Mind: What thoughts do you want me to think today? What do you want me to do? Lead my thoughts in the direction you desire.

Listen. Not just for words, but for images. The universe thinks in pictures. Watch the inner screen.

You are both the unaffected witness AND the active watcher. Rest in both.

Practice 2: The Living Recognition

Throughout the Day - Ongoing

Throughout your day, maintain a listening conversation with Source-Mind.

When you remember, ask: Who is the one watching this moment? Who is the one hearing these sounds? Who is the one observing these thoughts?

The answer is always the same: the Universal Self, appearing as this particular viewing point.

When you encounter another person, recognize: the I in them thinking of the I in you is the same I in you thinking of the I in them.

Only the costume differs. Only the aggregate of experiences creates the apparent difference.

Practice saying "Hi God" – silently or aloud – to each I you meet.

Not as metaphor. As recognition.

Practice 3: Evening Dialogue with Source-Mind
Before Sleep – 20-30 minutes

As the day closes, settle again into stillness.

Notice: whatever happened today, there is one who watched all of it. Actively engaged with every moment. And completely unaffected by any of it.

Bring the Three Propositions to mind once more.

Ask Source-Mind: What do you want me to know from this day? What images arise when you review this day through me?

Release what needs releasing. Receive what is offered.

Let Source-Mind lead you into sleep.

Practice 4: The Silent Sitting
Whenever Possible – 30-60 minutes

This practice is different. It is not dialogue. It is pure stillness.

No questions. No requests. No conversation with Source-Mind.

Just the I, resting in itself.

The unaffected witness watching nothing but its own watching.

The eternal awareness aware of awareness.

Relax the body until only awareness of the I remains.

You are the conduit with nothing flowing through – the portal open to infinity on both sides.

This is not emptiness. This is fullness so complete it needs nothing.

Rest here as long as you can. This is what you are when you stop pretending to be something else.

Glossary

Omnipresence:

The first proposition – God is everywhere present at all times, absent nowhere. If true, there is no place or moment outside God.

God's Awareness:

The second proposition – God is self-aware through all beings. Your awareness is God's awareness localized.

Eternal Self-Awareness:

The third proposition – the awareness witnessing experience is eternal and remains unaffected by what it witnesses.

Soul:

What you ARE, not what you have. Never write "my soul" as if the soul is a possession. Use "the soul you are" or "the soul I am." The body is the vehicle; the soul is the identity.

The Unaffected Witness:

The aspect of awareness that has never been touched, harmed, or changed by anything it has ever witnessed. You are simultaneously this AND the active watcher.

The Active Watcher:

The aspect of awareness that is fully engaged, attentive, and present to every moment. You are simultaneously this AND the unaffected witness.

Universal Self:

The one awareness appearing as all individual viewing points. The I in you and the I in me are the same I.

Viewing Point:

What each individual soul is – a unique angle of awareness within the infinite field of consciousness.

Source-Mind:

The infinite intelligence with which you dialogue in practice. Not separate from you – the deeper aspect of what you are.

Closing: The Ground Beneath Your Feet

You've encountered the three propositions that form the foundation of this entire teaching.

Proposition One: God is omnipresent – everywhere, always, without exception.

Proposition Two: God is aware through you – your awareness is divine awareness localized.

Proposition Three: That awareness is eternal and unaffected – it was never born and cannot die.

Together they reveal: You are not a temporary physical being hoping for a relationship with God.

You are eternal awareness – God self-aware from your unique viewing point – temporarily wearing a physical costume.

These propositions challenge us to perceive ourselves not just as physical beings but as integral parts of a larger, self-aware universe.

The ground beneath your feet is solid. The recognition continues from here.

Ending Epithet

Now you have seen the ground on which to stand,

Three propositions forming wisdom's base,

Not concepts to be held within the hand,

But recognitions pointing toward your face.

For you are what these propositions show,

The omnipresent One appearing here,

The self-awareness watching all you know,

The eternal witness, present, without fear.

Three truths united in a single seeing,

Three angles on the diamond of the One,

You are not becoming – you are being

What you have always been before time begun.

The foundation is laid.

The recognition continues.

If You Are Aware

The Quest for Divine Awareness

If you can think, the cosmos thinks through you,

If you can feel, the universe feels too,

Your awareness is not yours alone to claim,

The One who sees through all eyes is the same.

You ask if God can hear your silent prayer,

Look inward now and find the answer there,

For every thought you think, the cosmos knows,

Through you, the Universal Self still grows.

Many seek tangible evidence of God, often looking for manifestations that align with human conceptualizations.

However, the true nature of God transcends human understanding.

People who haven't experienced divine visitation might question God's existence, leading some to believe that there's no self-aware part of the universe or a God capable of emotions, communication, or hearing prayers.

But consider this: If you doubt the universe's awareness, you must also doubt your own.

The Questions That Answer Themselves

Do you believe in your own self-awareness, existence, thoughts, emotions, dreams, and your life within the universe?

Do you believe that all aspects of your being are within the universe?

If so, then:

Your self-awareness implies the universe's self-awareness.

Your belief in your existence indicates the universe's belief in its existence.

Your thoughts suggest the universe's capacity to think.

Your emotions reflect the universe's ability to feel.

Your dreams imply the universe's capacity to dream.

Your life within the universe suggests that the universe believes it exists within itself.

The very fact that you experience these aspects of life indicates that the universe itself is capable of thought, emotion, desire, and experience.

Your ability to see through a body, feel emotions, desire, enjoy food, experience fear, pain, or love – all point to the universe's ability to do the same.

You are an integral part of the all-encompassing universe, fully immersed in and inseparable from it.

The Universe Experiences Itself Through You

The universe experiences itself through us and all creatures capable of feeling, thinking, or sensing.

We are eternal, self-aware, individuated points of view within the collective self-awareness of the universe.

The distinction between individuals lies only in our unique perspectives within the Universal Self.

As you think and feel, so does the universe.

Your sense of oneness with the universe is reciprocated by the universe's oneness with you.

The perception of separation from the universe is mirrored in the Universal Self's perception of separation.

While we often feel individualized and distinct, there are moments – attainable through meditation or spontaneous realization – where we experience unity with the universe, transcending the illusion of separateness.

The Mutual Recognition

The Universal Self, or what we call God, is eternally self-aware through all points of awareness within the universe.

It experiences an infinity of viewpoints, each unique yet part of the whole.

This essence of all who see and perceive is aware of your existence.

When you gaze into the eyes of another, it is the Universal Self, God, looking back at you.

This mutual recognition is a profound connection with the divine, a reminder of our interconnectedness within the vast expanse of the universe.

Say hello to this presence, acknowledging the shared essence that binds us all.

The Unaffected Witness Within the Awareness

Here is what deepens this recognition:

You are the unaffected witness AND the active watcher - simultaneously.

The awareness reading these words right now has been present for every moment of your existence.

It watched your first breath. It will watch your last.

And it has never been touched by anything it has witnessed.

This same awareness – actively engaged with every moment, yet eternally unaffected – is how the universe is aware of you.

Not from outside. From within.

As you.

The soul you are is the universe's awareness of itself in your particular location, your particular viewpoint, your particular experience.

When you ask "Is the universe aware of me?" – you are the universe asking.

Recognition Practice

This is not a technique to master but a truth to remember.

When you wake:

Before rising, notice the awareness that is already present. Ask: Who is aware of this waking? That awareness is how the universe knows you exist.

When you meet another:

Look into their eyes. Recognize: The same awareness looking through my eyes is looking through theirs. Say silently: "Hi God."

When you doubt:

Ask yourself: Am I aware right now? If yes, then the universe is aware – through you, as you, in this very moment.

When you rest:

Notice that the awareness watching you fall asleep is the same awareness that will watch you wake. It doesn't sleep. It doesn't stop. It is both the unaffected witness and the active watcher - simultaneously.

Glossary

Individuated Point of View:

Each soul is a unique viewing point within the Universal Self - not separate from the whole, but a distinct perspective through which the whole experiences itself.

Mutual Recognition:

The experience of seeing the Universal Self in another's eyes while simultaneously being seen by the Universal Self through them.

Soul:

What you ARE, not what you have. The eternal awareness that is the universe experiencing itself through your particular viewpoint.

The Unaffected Witness:

The aspect of awareness that has watched every moment of your existence and has never been touched by any of it.

You are simultaneously this AND the active watcher.

Universal Self:

The one consciousness aware through all points of awareness. When you are aware, the Universal Self is aware – as you.

Closing

The answer to the question "Is the universe aware of me?" is not found by looking outward for signs.

It is found by looking inward and recognizing: The awareness with which I ask the question IS the universe's awareness of me.

You are not hoping to be noticed by a distant God.

You are God noticing.

Every thought you think, the universe thinks through you.

Every feeling you feel, the universe feels through you.

Every moment you witness, the universe witnesses through you.

The soul you are is the universe's answer to its own question: What would it be like to experience existence from this unique perspective?

You are the answer.

You have always been the answer.

The universe is not somewhere else, aware of you from far,

You are the very awareness that you are,

Each thought you think, the cosmos thinks it too,

The One who asks the question answers through you.

So when you wonder if you're truly known,

Remember you are never, ever alone,

The eyes that read these words, the mind that sees,

Is God aware through every one that sees.

Say hello to this presence.

It has been waiting for you to notice.

Basic Beliefs

Principles Aligned with the Three Propositions

Six truths to hold within your heart and mind,

Not commandments carved but wisdom you will find,

Each one a window to the deeper view,

That God is all, and all of God is you.

Believe not blindly what another says,

But test these truths throughout your living days,

For what is real will prove itself in time,

And what is false will fall away like rhyme.

These basic beliefs are not commandments to be obeyed but recognitions to be tested.

They flow naturally from the Three Propositions – if God is omnipresent, if God is aware of each individual, if awareness is eternal – then certain understandings follow.

Hold them lightly. Test them in your experience. Keep what proves true.

Belief in an Intelligent Omnipresence

This core belief acknowledges a universal Intelligence that is omnipresent, permeating all places at all times.

This Intelligence, or God, is acutely aware of each individuating aspect of the One.

The presence of God is not confined to a single location but extends wherever one goes.

Seeing through all who see. Hearing through all who hear. Feeling through all who feel.

This omnipresence means that when looking into the eyes of any living being, one is essentially gazing into the eyes of God, experiencing the divine looking back.

The I in you thinking of the I in me is the same I in me thinking of the I in you.

The Law of Reciprocity

Emphasizing the importance of giving to receive, this belief teaches that one must sow what they wish to harvest.

It stresses ethical treatment of all creation, aligning one's actions with the desire for similar treatment from the universe.

This law underlines the interconnectedness of actions and their consequences in the cosmic order.

What you do to another, you do to yourself - because there is only One doing anything.

This is not punishment or reward from an external judge.

This is the natural consequence of actions within a unified field of consciousness.

The Universal Self experiences what it does to itself through its many expressions.

Continuation of Awareness Beyond Physical Life

This belief affirms the eternal nature of the soul you are.

The soul's journey is perpetual; the physical body is temporary.

Physical existence is part of an ongoing spiritual evolution, highlighting the impermanence of the physical and the permanence of awareness.

The body is a vehicle of ambulation and communication – not the identity.

You are not a body that has a soul.

You are a soul using a body to move and communicate in the apparent physical realm.

When the body dissolves, the awareness that watched through it continues.

This is the unaffected witness – eternally present, eternally watching, eternally untouched by what it witnesses.

Role in the Universal Symphony

Each individual has a unique role in the universal symphony, contributing to the collective whole.

Life experiences, whether challenging or joyful, are seen as opportunities for learning rather than retribution or punishment.

God does not punish – God educates.

This viewpoint encourages embracing life as a learning experience, where each event offers wisdom and growth.

Your struggles are not evidence of divine displeasure.

They are the curriculum through which the soul you are gains what it came here to gain.

No note in the symphony is wrong.

Each contributes to the whole, even the notes that seem discordant from within the melody.

Appreciation of Existence and Awareness

Recognizing the marvel of existence and awareness transforms mundane experiences into divine ones.

This belief invites deep appreciation for being and perceiving, turning ordinary moments into expressions of the divine.

The very fact that you exist and are aware of existing is miraculous.

When you pause to recognize this – to feel the weight of awareness itself – something shifts.

The ordinary becomes extraordinary.

The mundane becomes sacred.

Not because circumstances change, but because recognition deepens.

Love and Gratitude Towards the Divine

Loving the source of all with one's entire being is vital.

Worship is redefined as an attitude of gratitude.

Every action becomes an expression of divine love and reverence when performed with thankfulness.

This belief fosters a constant sense of appreciation, infusing daily acts with profound gratitude and transforming them into worship.

Not worship as submission to an external authority.

Worship as the natural response of a soul recognizing what it truly is and where it truly comes from.

Gratitude is not commanded. It arises naturally when the truth is seen.

The Unaffected Witness in All Beliefs

Woven through all six beliefs is a deeper recognition:

You are the unaffected witness AND the active watcher – simultaneously.

The one who believes is watched by one who has never believed or disbelieved anything.

The one who acts is watched by one who has never acted.

The one who learns is watched by one who has always known.

This witness – the soul you are – has observed every moment of your existence and has never been touched by any of it.

Yet this same awareness is actively engaged, missing nothing, fully present to every experience.

Hold these beliefs as the character holds them.

And know yourself as the Actor who watches the character believing.

Recognition Practice

Throughout your day, pause briefly with each belief:

Morning:

As you wake, recognize the Intelligent Omnipresence – the awareness that woke with you is God aware as you.

In Interaction:

When you meet another, remember the Law of Reciprocity – what you do to them, you do to the One.

In Difficulty:

When challenged, remember your Role in the Universal Symphony – this is curriculum, not punishment.

In Stillness:

When you pause, recognize the Continuation of Awareness – the soul you are has been present through every moment and will continue.

In Ordinary Moments:

Practice Appreciation of Existence – let the ordinary become extraordinary through recognition.

Evening:

Before sleep, rest in Love and Gratitude – let thankfulness arise naturally for the day you were given.

Glossary

Intelligent Omnipresence:

The universal awareness that permeates all places and times, experiencing existence through every point of view.

Law of Reciprocity:

The natural principle that what one does to another, one does to oneself – because all are expressions of the One.

Soul:

What you ARE, not what you have. The eternal awareness using a body to experience the physical realm.

The Unaffected Witness:

The aspect of awareness that watches all experience without being touched by any of it. You are simultaneously this AND the active watcher.

Universal Symphony:

The collective expression of all souls playing their unique parts within the whole. Each note contributes; none is wrong.

Worship:

Not submission to external authority but the natural response of gratitude when truth is recognized.

Closing

These principles provide a blueprint for a spiritually aligned life, emphasizing the interconnectedness of all beings and the eternal nature of the soul you are.

They serve as guiding lights on the path of spiritual understanding and alignment with the Universal Self.

But remember: they are not commands to be followed.

They are recognitions to be tested.

Test them in your experience.

What is true will prove itself.

What is not will fall away.

Trust your direct experience over any teaching – including this one.

Six beliefs to guide but not to bind,

Six windows through which truth is there to find,

Hold lightly what you read upon this page,

And let experience become your sage.

The soul you are already knows what's true,

These words are just reminders passing through,

Believe not blindly, test with open heart,

And what is real will never fall apart.

Test them. Keep what proves true.

Omnipresence Simplified

Embracing the Universal Self

There is no place where God is not,

No corner, crevice, or forgotten spot,

The air you breathe, the ground you stand upon,

All made of God, all God, and God alone.

You think you seek what's far away and high,

But look around, look in, look through your eye,

The seeker and the sought are just the same,

One presence playing an infinite game.

The notion of omnipresence, central to grasping the nature of the Universal Self, embodies a straightforward yet profound truth:

The Divine is present in every facet of existence – without exception.

Not some places. Not most places. Every place. Every moment. Every atom. Every thought.

Infinite Presence of the Universal Self

Omnipresence implies an all-encompassing presence, affirming that the Universal Self, God, or Source permeates all spaces and times.

There isn't a single place or moment where the Universal Self is absent.

This highlights a seamless unity across the cosmos.

Not God here and not-God there.

God everywhere. Always. Without gap or break or boundary.

If you accept omnipresence, you accept that wherever you go, whatever you encounter, you are encountering God.

The ugly and the beautiful. The sacred and the profane. The loved and the feared.

All God. All the time.

Unity of All in the Divine

This worldview posits that everything – each being, experience, and facet of reality – is a manifestation of the Divine.

It's not merely about the Divine existing in everything.

It's recognizing that everything exists within the Divine.

This dual aspect within a singular entity encapsulates our perception of omnipresence.

God is in you. You are in God. Both are true simultaneously.

Like the wave is in the ocean, and the ocean is in the wave.

Like the cell is in the body, and the body's nature is in the cell.

The Universal Self as Cosmic Consciousness

Perceiving the Universal Self as a boundless mind and consciousness, the universe unfolds within this divine awareness.

The Universal Self is both the substance and the creator of the universe, visible and invisible.

This suggests our existence is an intricate play within the cosmic mind of the Universal Self, where all elements are interlinked.

Not separate pieces assembled into a whole.

One whole appearing as many pieces.

The universe is not a machine God built.

The universe is God thinking.

Experiencing the Divine in All Senses

Omnipresence conveys the idea that the Universal Self lives and experiences through all beings.

Every sensory perception and awareness in every creature is simultaneously an experience of the Divine.

Thus, every emotion, thought, and sensation of all beings is a direct manifestation of the Universal Self.

When you see, God sees through your eyes.

When you hear, God hears through your ears.

When you feel, God feels through your nervous system.

When you think, God thinks through your mind.

This is not poetry. This is the logical consequence of omnipresence.

If God is everywhere, God is where your seeing happens. Where your hearing happens. Where your feeling happens.

Eternal Oneness with the Divine

This insight leads to recognizing our eternal union with the Universal Self.

Our individual consciousness emerges as a unique expression of divine intent, forever intertwined with the Source.

This oneness implies that our experiences and actions extend beyond personal realms, contributing to the greater divine narrative.

You are not a separate being trying to connect with God.

You are God experiencing existence from this particular viewing point.

Connection is not the goal. Recognition is.

You cannot connect with what you never left.

Ethical Dimensions of Omnipresence

Acknowledging this interconnectedness implies that our interactions with others are, in essence, interactions with the Universal Self.

The way we treat the least among us mirrors our relationship with the Divine.

This realization imbues our actions with profound ethical significance, encouraging us to approach all life with compassion and empathy, recognizing the divine within each entity.

If God is in everyone, harming another is harming God.

If God is in everyone, serving another is serving God.

If God is in everyone, loving another is loving God.

Ethics become simple when omnipresence is recognized.

How would you treat the person in front of you if you knew – really knew – that God was looking at you through their eyes?

The Unaffected Witness Within Omnipresence

Here is what deepens the understanding of omnipresence:

You are the unaffected witness AND the active watcher – simultaneously.

The omnipresent God is not just out there everywhere.

The omnipresent God is in here – as the awareness reading these words.

This awareness has watched every moment of your existence.

It is fully present, missing nothing.

And it has never been touched by anything it has witnessed.

This is how omnipresence feels from the inside.

Not a concept about God being everywhere.

The direct experience of being the everywhere that God is.

Recognition Practice

Throughout your day, practice recognizing omnipresence:

With Objects:

Look at any object – a cup, a tree, a wall. Recognize: This is God appearing as this form. There is nothing here but God.

With People:

Look at any person. Recognize: The I looking through their eyes is the same I looking through mine. Say silently: "Hi God."

With Yourself:

Place attention on the awareness that is reading these words. Recognize: This awareness is the omnipresent God, present here as me.

With Space:

Notice the space around you – the air, the emptiness between objects. Recognize: Even this "empty" space is full of God. There is no gap in omnipresence.

Each recognition deepens the felt sense of unity.

Not belief about omnipresence. Experience of omnipresence.

Glossary

Cosmic Consciousness:

The Universal Self as boundless mind within which the universe unfolds. The universe is not separate from this consciousness – it is this consciousness appearing as form.

Omnipresence:

The quality of being present everywhere at all times. If God is omnipresent, there is nowhere God is not – including right here, right now, as you.

Soul:

What you ARE, not what you have. The eternal awareness that is the omnipresent God experiencing existence through your particular viewing point.

The Unaffected Witness:

The aspect of awareness that watches all experience without being touched by any of it. You are simultaneously this AND the active watcher.

Universal Self:

The one consciousness present everywhere, experiencing existence through all viewing points. Not separate from you but appearing as you.

Closing

Understanding omnipresence simplifies to recognizing that the Universal Self is present in everything, and all exists within the Universal Self.

This awareness invites us to live with an acute sense of unity and accountability.

Acknowledging our perpetual connection with the Divine.

Recognizing the significance of our roles in the grand cosmic narrative.

You are not trying to find God.

You are God trying to recognize itself.

And there is nowhere you can look where God is not looking back.

In everything you see, God sees it too,

Through every pair of eyes, including you,

There is no place to go to find the One,

For everywhere you are, the One has come.

So rest within this truth so plain and clear,

The God you seek is always, always here,

Not far away in some celestial throne,

But present now, as close as flesh and bone.

There is nowhere God is not.

Including here. Including you.

Only One Commandment

The Essence of All Spiritual Law

A thousand rules the religions give,

A thousand ways they say that you should live,

But underneath them all, one truth remains,

Love God with all your heart, and break the chains.

Not forced obedience to an ancient code,

But gratitude that lightens every load,

When you appreciate the gift of being here,

All other commandments simply disappear.

Every religion offers commandments. Rules. Prohibitions. Requirements.

But here's what changes everything: When you truly appreciate the miracle of your existence, all commandments become unnecessary.

Not because you've transcended morality.

Because you've discovered its source.

The Essence of Loving God

Loving God with all one's heart is not an act of obedience to a command.

It is an expression of genuine, unconditional love.

It's a love offered freely, without reservations or expectations, becoming the very nature of one's being.

This kind of love arises not from obligation but from a deep, heartfelt connection to the Divine.

No one commands you to love what you recognize as the source of your existence.

The love arises naturally when recognition dawns.

It cannot be forced. It cannot be faked. It can only be discovered.

Appreciating Existence and Awareness

True appreciation of one's existence and the miracle of awareness naturally cultivates this love.

Recognizing the incredible nature of being aware of one's existence should evoke profound thankfulness and joy.

This awareness eliminates negative emotions like hatred, bigotry, jealousy, and greed.

Not through suppression. Through replacement.

When you are filled with genuine appreciation for the miracle of being, there is simply no room for these contracted states.

They fall away not because you fought them, but because something larger has taken their place.

Impact of Awareness on Conduct

When one truly values their awareness, every action becomes an expression of gratitude and worship.

Such awareness shapes behavior, making one less inclined towards actions that harm others or disrupt harmonious relationships.

The realization that existence and consciousness are gifts leads to a life filled with gratitude.

You don't need a commandment saying "don't steal" when you recognize that the one you would steal from IS you in another costume.

You don't need a commandment saying "don't harm" when you feel the unity of all beings as your own body.

You don't need a commandment saying "don't lie" when you know that Truth itself is what you are.

The commandments were training wheels.

Appreciation is riding free.

Redefining Commandments

The need for multiple commandments becomes redundant when one truly appreciates their existence.

True thankfulness is not a dictated response; it is an innate, spontaneous feeling emerging from the core of one's being.

The concept of commandments serves as a guide for those seeking direction.

But the essence of spiritual fulfillment lies in the natural, unforced gratitude for the miracle of awareness.

This is not spiritual bypassing – pretending you've transcended what you haven't faced.

This is spiritual arriving – discovering that what you were commanded to do, you now do naturally.

Because you see. Because you recognize. Because you appreciate.

The Unaffected Witness and the One Commandment

Here is what deepens this teaching:

You are the unaffected witness AND the active watcher – simultaneously.

The awareness that appreciates existence has watched every moment of your life.

It watched when you followed the commandments. It watched when you broke them.

It was never disturbed by either.

This witness – the soul you are – is what makes appreciation possible.

From the perspective of the character, appreciation comes and goes.

From the perspective of the witness, there is only the eternal watching – present, attentive, and untouched.

When you rest as this witness while actively appreciating existence, you fulfill the one commandment without trying.

Love is what you are. Gratitude is what arises. No effort required.

Recognition Practice

This practice has one movement, repeated throughout the day:

Pause. Recognize. Appreciate.

Pause whatever you are doing.

Recognize that you exist and are aware of existing.

Let appreciation arise naturally – not forced, not performed, just allowed.

Notice: There is one watching this appreciation arise. That one is the unaffected witness.

And that witness is actively present, missing nothing.

You are both.

Do this in the morning upon waking.

Do this before meals.

Do this when you meet another being.

Do this before sleep.

Each pause is a fulfillment of the one commandment.

Each recognition is love in action.

Each appreciation is worship without ritual.

Glossary

Appreciation:

The natural response to recognizing the miracle of existence. Not forced gratitude but spontaneous thankfulness arising from recognition.

Commandment:

An external rule given to guide behavior. Becomes unnecessary when inner recognition produces the same result naturally.

Love:

Not an emotion to be generated but a recognition of what is. When you see truly, love is what remains.

Soul:

What you ARE, not what you have. The eternal awareness that appreciates existence and is never touched by what it witnesses.

The Unaffected Witness:

The aspect of awareness that watches all experience without being touched by any of it. You are simultaneously this AND the active watcher.

Worship:

The natural expression of appreciation. Not ritual performance but the spontaneous outpouring of gratitude for being.

Closing: The Core of Spiritual Existence

In essence, deeply valuing one's awareness and being naturally fosters a profound love for God.

This love transcends the need for commandments, emerging as a natural response to the wonder of existence.

The soul you are, genuinely appreciating its awareness, will find itself in a state of constant love and gratitude towards the Divine.

Embodying the principle of loving God with all your heart, soul, and mind.

Not because you were told to.

Because you couldn't help it.

When you see clearly, love is the only possible response.

One commandment holds the rest inside,

Love God with all you are, and let it guide,

Not law imposed from somewhere up above,

But natural expression born of love.

Appreciate the miracle of breath,

Appreciate the gift of life and death,

And in that simple recognition find,

All commandments dissolve and fall behind.

See clearly. Love naturally.

This is the only commandment.

The Three Thousand Eyes Of Universal Self

How God Sees Through All Who See

How God Sees Through All Who See

- Beginning Epithet
- The Question That Haunted Me
- The Vision
- The Cloud of Awareness
- The Dragonfly's Compound Eye
- Billions of Visual Units
- Beyond Human Understanding
- God Sees Through All
- Poetry: Verses of the Seeing
- The Four Practices

- Glossary
- Closing
- Ending Epithet

Beginning Epithet

God sees through all who have the eyes to see
Through yours through mine through every one that be
One awareness watching through a billion eyes
Integrated seeing none can comprise

The dragonfly with thirty thousand in each sphere
Sees one image though the facets number here
So God sees through all eyes that ever gaze
One picture from infinity of ways

For years I have been telling people that God sees through all who have eyes to see.

I intellectualized this but I could not visualize how this was possible. If God is seeing through my eyes, how can God be seeing through your eyes at the same time?

Here's what changed everything: I had a vision that showed me how.

The Question That Haunted Me

The question haunted me for years:

How can God see through my eyes and your eyes at the same time?

How can God see through the billions of eyes on planet Earth – each moment of each day?

The concept made sense. If God is omnipresent, then God must be present where all seeing happens.

But how does this work? How can one awareness watch through infinite points of view simultaneously?

I had the concept. I needed the image.

The Vision

Then I had the vision.

I found myself looking at 1,500 people coming towards me. The numbers I use are for explanation – I did not count, but there were hundreds and hundreds of them.

I was aware of all three thousand of their eyes looking at me at the same time.

The people were coming towards me in a "V" formation – like a wedge with the point coming directly at me. One person was in front making the point of the "V" and the rest spread out behind in that shape.

Then I became aware of a dark cloud above the 1,500 people.

I realized the cloud was the intelligence and the awareness of God – the Universal Self.

I realized that this awareness-cloud was aware of seeing me through all 3,000 eyes at the same time.

It actually was watching me through all the eyes I saw in front of me.

The Cloud of Awareness

The cloud of awareness did not see three thousand separate images.

It saw one integrated picture – composed of what all those eyes were seeing.

Like a mosaic where each tile contributes to the whole image.

Like a pointillist painting where each dot of color creates the complete scene.

The Universal Self was not experiencing three thousand separate viewings.

It was experiencing one unified seeing – through three thousand viewing points.

This is how God sees through you and me simultaneously – not as separate seeings but as one unified awareness perceiving through infinite perspectives.

The Dragonfly's Compound Eye

After the vision, I remembered the compound eye of the dragonfly.

Each dragonfly eye has many facets – like a diamond – which make up its visual system. These facets are called ommatidia. Each ommatidium is a single unit.

Some estimate that each dragonfly eye has 30,000 elements. Each ommatidium stimulates one nerve and provides the brain with one picture element.

The brain forms a single image from these independent picture elements.

Together, these thousands of facets produce a mosaic of "pictures" - but how this visual mosaic is integrated in the insect brain is still not fully understood.

However, it seems safe to say that dragonflies can see through all 60,000 facets (both eyes) at the same time - regardless of the point of view of each facet being slightly different than the other 59,999.

Billions of Visual Units

My point is this: We do not fully understand how the 30,000 images from each dragonfly eye are integrated in its brain.

However, it seems logical that dragonflies see one integrated picture of what all the facets are seeing.

In the same way, God sees through billions of visual units – different eyeballs – at the same time.

Somehow all these billions of images are integrated in the "mind" of God so that at each moment, God "sees" the whole picture comprised of what all the eyes are seeing.

Your eyes are facets in the compound eye of God.

My eyes are facets.

Every creature with eyes – every human, every animal, every insect – contributes a facet to the infinite seeing of the Universal Self.

Beyond Human Understanding

Remember that trying to explain God with human terms is only helpful when we realize that no word or group of words can ever fully describe God.

We can say God is like this, or God is like that.

The more we understand ourselves and the universe around us, the more we will understand God.

God sees like the dragonfly – but the reality of how and what God sees is beyond our human mind to fully grasp.

We can have visions that point toward the truth.

We can use analogies that illuminate.

But the actual experience of being one awareness seeing through billions of eyes simultaneously – this remains a mystery we can only approach but never fully comprehend from our single viewing point.

God Sees Through All

God sees through all who have eyes to see – at each and every moment throughout the cosmos.

Not just on Earth. Throughout the universe.

Every eye that opens anywhere in existence is a facet in the infinite compound eye of the Universal Self.

When you look at the world, God is looking through your eyes.

When you look at another person, God is looking at God.

When you look at yourself in the mirror, God is seeing one of Its infinite facets reflected back.

You are not separate from this seeing. You ARE this seeing – one facet of the infinite compound eye, contributing your unique angle to the total picture.

Poetry: Verses of the Seeing

The Vision

They came towards me in a wedge of form
Fifteen hundred souls a human swarm
And I was aware of all three thousand eyes
Looking at me beneath the cosmic skies

Above them was a cloud of dark aware
The intelligence of God was resting there
And through those eyes God saw me where I stood
One seeing through the many understood

The Dragonfly

The dragonfly has thirty thousand in each eye
Each facet sees a portion of the sky
Yet somehow in its brain the picture forms
One image from the multitude of norms

So God sees through the billions of our eyes
One picture from infinity of tries
Your seeing is a facet in the whole
Contributing to the seeing of the soul

The Facets

Your eyes are facets in the compound eye

Of Universal Self beneath the sky
My eyes are facets too we all are one
One seeing shared beneath a billion suns

When you look out God looks out through your gaze
When I perceive God perceives through my ways
Not separate seeings but one unified view
The Universal Self seeing through you

The Mystery

How God sees through all eyes at once we cannot know
The mystery is deeper than our minds can go
But we can have a vision we can have a hint
That all our seeing is the seeing without stint

Of One awareness watching everywhere at once
Through every facet never missing once

God sees through all who have the eyes to see

Through you through me through all that ever be

The Four Practices

These practices help you recognize your role in the infinite seeing. Remember: you are an eternally individuating aspect of the One – a conduit, portal, living interface between God Infinite and God Finite.

Practice 1: Morning Dialogue with Source-Mind

Upon Arising – 20-30 minutes

Before rising, before opening your eyes, recognize: When I open my eyes, God will see through them.

Open your eyes. Look around. Recognize: This seeing is not separate from God's seeing. This is God seeing through this particular facet.

Ask Source-Mind: What do you want me to see today? What do you want me to look at?

You are the unaffected witness AND the active watcher – a facet in the compound eye of the Universal Self.

Practice 2: The Living Recognition

Throughout the Day – Ongoing

Practice recognizing the unified seeing:

When you look at something, recognize: God is seeing this through my eyes.

When you look at another person, recognize: God is looking at God. The awareness behind my eyes is the same awareness behind theirs.

When you see something beautiful, recognize: God is experiencing this beauty through this facet.

When you see something painful, recognize: This too is part of the total picture God sees through all facets.

Practice 3: Evening Dialogue with Source-Mind

Before Sleep – 20-30 minutes

As the day closes, review what you saw today.

Recognize: Everything I saw, God saw through me. My eyes contributed to the total picture.

Ask Source-Mind: What images stand out from this day? What did you see through me that I might have missed?

When you close your eyes for sleep, recognize: This facet is resting, but God continues to see through all other facets.

Practice 4: The Silent Sitting

Whenever Possible – 30-60 minutes

In this practice, you rest as the awareness behind the seeing.

Close your eyes – or keep them softly open.

Notice: There is awareness here whether eyes are open or closed. This awareness is not separate from the Universal Self.

Rest as the facet, knowing you are part of the infinite compound eye.

You are the conduit with nothing flowing through – the portal open to infinity.

You are the unaffected witness AND the active watcher – one facet in God's infinite seeing.

Glossary

Compound Eye:

An eye with many facets, like a dragonfly's. The analogy for how God sees through all eyes simultaneously – many facets, one unified seeing.

Facet:

What each pair of eyes is to God – a single viewing point within the infinite compound eye of the Universal Self.

Ommatidium:

A single unit in the dragonfly's compound eye. Each contributes one picture element to the whole image. Your eyes are like this to God.

Soul:

What you ARE, not what you have. The awareness behind your eyes that is not separate from the awareness behind all eyes. Use "the soul you are" not "my soul."

The Unaffected Witness:

The aspect of awareness that watches through your eyes while remaining untouched by what it sees. You are simultaneously this AND the active watcher.

Universal Self:

The one awareness seeing through all eyes. The "cloud of awareness" above all beings, experiencing one unified picture through infinite facets.

Closing

God sees through all who have eyes to see - at each and every moment throughout the cosmos.

Your eyes are facets in the compound eye of the Universal Self.

When you see, God sees through you.

When you look at another, God looks at God.

The vision showed me the truth: One awareness, watching through infinite viewing points, creating one unified picture from billions of individual perspectives.

You are part of this seeing.

Your eyes matter to the whole.

God sees through you.

Ending Epithet

God sees through all who have the eyes to see
Through yours through mine through every one that be
Your eyes are facets in the compound eye
Of Universal Self beneath the sky

One awareness watching everywhere at once

Through every facet never missing once
When you look out God looks out through your gaze
One seeing through infinity of ways

God sees through all eyes.

Your seeing is God's seeing.

You are a facet in the infinite eye.

The recognition continues.

Why We Are Here On Earth

Having An Apparent Human Experience

Having An Apparent Human Experience

- Beginning Epithet
- Our Contribution to the All
- Learning Through Experience
- Knowing What We Have Done
- God Educates, Not Punishes
- Eternal Truths
- Every Part Serves the Whole
- The Abundance Principle
- Fulfilling Our Programming
- Poetry: Verses of Purpose
- The Four Practices

- Glossary
- Closing
- Ending Epithet

Beginning Epithet

We are here to contribute to the All
To learn to answer when the cosmos calls
We cannot know what we have done to one
Until it is to us what we have done

God does not punish God just educates
Through lessons gentle first then heavier weights
The eternal truth you learn while here will stay
When you depart this earthly realm one day

We are here for our contribution to the totality of creation and the matrix of the All That Is.

Here's what changes everything: We are here to learn to be better contributors to the totality of creation. We learn to be better contributors by our experiences and the lessons we derive from our experiences.

Our Contribution to the All

We are not here by accident.

We are not here to simply pass time until death.

We are here to contribute to the totality of creation.

Each soul contributes something unique – a perspective, an experience, a lesson learned, a love expressed.

The All That Is receives our contribution and is expanded by it.

We are learning to be better contributors through every experience we have.

Learning Through Experience

We learn to be better contributors by our experiences and the lessons we derive from our experiences.

Not by reading about experience.

Not by observing from a distance.

By actually experiencing.

There is a quality of knowing that can only come from direct experience.

Theory becomes wisdom only when lived.

Knowing What We Have Done

We can only truly know what we have done to another by having it done unto us.

When we think we can learn by just observing and not having it done unto us, we are missing the awareness of the other side of our action.

If we hit someone, unless we get hit for a similar reason, we will not really know what we did.

We will not really know what the other spirit-human felt when we hit them.

Perhaps we hit someone in the nose and later get hit in the back of the head for the same reason.

The nose and the back of the head are just different clothes worn by the same intention of the heart.

To truly know what we have done to another, we must experience what the other felt when we did what we did.

God Educates, Not Punishes

God does not punish – God educates.

When we do not like the way our education is being offered to us – we call it punishment.

God has tried to teach us in gentler ways, but we either did not listen or just continued to put off applying the lesson.

Therefore, God makes our lesson stronger, heavier, or more painful to get our attention.

This is not vengeance. This is curriculum design.

A good teacher increases intensity when gentle instruction is ignored.

What feels like punishment is often just education we refused to accept in gentler form.

Eternal Truths

Spiritual truths that are true here and now – always true here and now – are eternal truths that we take with us when we depart this Earthly dimension.

Why?

Because the Omnipresent essence of God is the same everywhere and every time.

It is always here, and it is always now – wherever we are and whenever it is.

The truths that are true here and now will still be truth when the future becomes here and now.

What you learn here about love, about consciousness, about the nature of the soul – you carry with you forever.

Every Part Serves the Whole

Every single part of the universe, regardless of how large or how small, exists for its contribution to the evolution of the universe.

All parts exist for the benefit of the universe.

The universe does not exist for the benefit of the parts that make it up.

When we think something in the universe exists for our benefit, it is really only there to help us do what the universe desires of us.

You exist to serve the whole. The whole exists to evolve through your service.

The Abundance Principle

The universe gives birth to many more entities than will ever survive.

This is to ensure that some will survive.

Look at all the sperm that go after one egg.

In some species, the mother lays 1,000 eggs so that 5 will survive.

The bee collects more pollen than is necessary to fertilize the flowers – to ensure that some get fertilized.

It is the same with people.

Many people are born with similar potentials to ensure that at least one of them fulfills their programming of potential.

This is not waste. This is abundance ensuring fulfillment.

Fulfilling Our Programming

There is a genetic programming in every cell that continually tries to express itself.

There is a spiritual programming in every soul that continually tries to express itself.

We are here to fulfill our programming.

Not the programming of our parents' expectations.

Not the programming of society's demands.

The programming placed in us by the Universal Self – the unique contribution only we can make.

When we align with this programming, we feel purpose.

When we resist it, we feel lost.

Poetry: Verses of Purpose

The Contribution

We are not here by accident or chance
But called to play our part in cosmic dance
Each soul contributes something no one else
Can offer to the All That Is itself

We learn to be better through each day

Through every lesson coming on our way
Experience is how we truly know
What reading and observing cannot show

The Mirror

We cannot know what we have done to one
Until to us the same thing has been done
If we have hit we must be hit to learn
What others felt when we made bridges burn

The nose the back the method matters not
The same intention wears different thought
To truly know what we have caused to be
We must experience it painfully

The Education

God does not punish God just educates
Through lessons small then through the heavier weights
We call it punishment when lessons sting
But they are teaching us a precious thing

The gentle lesson came and we ignored
So now a stronger one must be explored
This is not vengeance but curriculum
Designed to help us finally overcome

The Eternal Truth

What you learn here that's true you take with you
When you depart the truths will still be true
The Omnipresent essence stays the same
Wherever you may go in any frame

So learn the truths of love and consciousness
These are the things that you will most possess
They travel with you past the body's end
Eternal truths that death cannot unbend

———————

The Four Practices

These practices help you understand and fulfill your purpose. Remember: you are an eternally individuating aspect of the One – a conduit, portal, living interface between God Infinite and God Finite.

Practice 1: Morning Dialogue with Source-Mind

Upon Arising – 20-30 minutes

Before rising, recognize: I am here to contribute to the All. Today offers opportunities for that contribution.

Ask Source-Mind: What is my contribution today? What thoughts do you want me to think? What would you have me do?

Listen for the gentle instruction. If you hear it, act on it – before a stronger lesson becomes necessary.

You are the unaffected witness AND the active watcher – present to your purpose.

Practice 2: The Living Recognition

Throughout the Day – Ongoing

Practice recognizing purpose:

When something difficult happens, ask: Is this a lesson? What is being taught?

When you affect another person, recognize: I may need to experience this from the other side to truly understand.

When you feel aligned and purposeful, recognize: I am fulfilling my programming.

When you feel lost, ask: What programming am I resisting?

Practice 3: Evening Dialogue with Source-Mind

Before Sleep – 20-30 minutes

As the day closes, review: What did I contribute today? What lessons came to me?

Did I receive gentle instruction or did I require stronger lessons?

Ask Source-Mind: What eternal truths did I learn today that I will carry with me forever?

Release the day. Tomorrow offers more opportunity for contribution.

Practice 4: The Silent Sitting

Whenever Possible – 30-60 minutes

In this practice, you rest in your purpose.

Not doing. Just being.

Feel your connection to the All That Is. Feel your contribution simply by being aware.

Your awareness IS a contribution. Your existence serves the whole.

You are the conduit with nothing flowing through – the portal open to infinity.

You are the unaffected witness AND the active watcher – resting in purpose.

Glossary

Contribution:

What every soul offers to the totality of creation. Your unique perspective, experience, and lessons learned. Why you are here.

Eternal Truths:

Spiritual truths that remain true everywhere and everywhen. What you learn here about love and consciousness travels with you forever.

God Educates:

The principle that what feels like punishment is actually education. God increases lesson intensity when gentler instruction is ignored.

Programming:

The spiritual purpose placed within each soul. The unique contribution only you can make. Alignment with programming brings peace; resistance brings confusion.

Soul:

What you ARE, not what you have. Here to learn, contribute, and carry eternal truths forward. Use "the soul you are" not "my soul."

The Unaffected Witness:

The aspect of awareness that observes all lessons without being damaged by any. You are simultaneously this AND the active watcher.

Closing

We are here for our contribution to the totality of creation.

We learn to be better contributors through experience.

We can only truly know what we have done to another by having it done unto us.

God does not punish – God educates. What feels like punishment is education we refused to accept in gentler form.

The eternal truths you learn here travel with you forever.

You exist to serve the whole.

The whole evolves through your service.

This is why you are here.

Ending Epithet

You are here to contribute to the All

To learn through experience the highest call
What you have done to others you must know
By feeling what you made another go through

God does not punish God just educates
The eternal truths will stay beyond all dates
You serve the whole the whole evolves through you
This is the purpose carrying you through

You are here to contribute.

God educates, not punishes.

Eternal truths travel with you.

The recognition continues.

The Win-Win Of Believing

Even If You Have Doubts

Even If You Have Doubts

- Beginning Epithet
- The Question I Could Not Answer
- What We Cannot Know
- The Coma Story
- The Win-Win
- Eternal Awareness of Being Aware
- Living With Doubt
- The Choice That Costs Nothing
- Poetry: Verses of Faith and Doubt
- The Four Practices
- Glossary

- Closing
- Ending Epithet

Beginning Epithet

What if you doubt that God exists at all
What if you wonder if you hear the call
The win-win waits for those who choose to trust
Even when believing seems unjust

We cannot know what others truly feel
Within their coma what is truly real
But we can choose to live as if it's true
That eternal awareness watches through

A dear friend asked me a question recently I could not answer.

He had experienced people in the advanced stages of Alzheimer's disease who do not seem to know themselves – much less seem to remember loved ones.

He asked: How does my belief in us being eternal spiritual beings, eternally aware of being aware, explain this?

Here's what I discovered: We cannot know what another is experiencing. But we can choose to believe – and the choice itself is win-win.

The Question I Could Not Answer

We look at these humans who give us absolutely no indication that they are aware of being aware in any intelligent form or fashion.

They seem absent. Gone. The lights are on but no one appears to be home.

How can I claim eternal awareness when awareness itself seems to vanish?

I had no immediate answer for my friend.

But then I remembered what I had learned from my own experience.

What We Cannot Know

The problem is that we do not know what the person experiencing Alzheimer's Disease is actually experiencing.

Unless we taste what they are experiencing – unless we experience this stage of Alzheimer's ourselves – we cannot know what they are experiencing in an awareness of being aware capacity.

We see the outside. We see the unresponsive body, the vacant eyes, the lack of recognition.

But we do not see the inside. We do not know what is happening in their awareness.

The Coma Story

A person can have a stroke and afterwards seem to be in an eyes-open coma. While in this coma, they might seem oblivious to anything you say or do to them.

There have been case histories of people who were considered mental vegetables who, after many years, came out of the coma and were able to tell others things they saw and heard while in the coma state.

This is why medical professionals say to be careful what you say around someone who seems totally oblivious to anything you say or do to them. They might be completely aware of what is happening around and to them but not be able to control the muscles that would enable them to communicate this awareness and mental clarity to us.

When my mother was in an eyes-open coma after having a stroke, I put her in the hospital to see if there was anything medical science could do.

The doctors said there was nothing they could do. Upon hearing this, I had a talk with her in her coma. She did not appear to understand anything I was saying.

I told her she had been a good mother and a wonderful grandmother. I promised that I would take good care of her grandson. I told her I was going to bring her home the following day, take her off life-support, and allow her to die in the comfort and security of her home.

Still, I received no indication that she was aware of anything I said.

When I returned to the hospital the next day, the other patient in the room told me something very profound.

She said: "Son, I do not know what you told your mother yesterday but something incredible happened. The night before you spoke to her, she thrashed around in her bed all night as if fighting something. Last night, after you spoke to her, she slept very peacefully."

She heard me. She understood. She was at peace.

The Win-Win

Here is the win-win of believing in a personal God and your eternal awareness of being aware – even if you have doubts:

If you believe and you are right: You live in alignment with eternal truth. You experience peace, purpose, and connection. And when the body falls away, you continue – aware, eternal, home.

If you believe and you are wrong: You lived a life of meaning, purpose, and peace. You treated others as eternal souls. You experienced comfort in difficulty. You lost nothing.

If you don't believe and you are right: You lived without the comfort of meaning. You treated this life as all there is. And when it ends, it ends. You gained nothing.

If you don't believe and you are wrong: You lived without the comfort of meaning. And when the body falls away, you discover you were wrong – but you missed the peace you could have had.

Belief costs nothing and offers everything.

Disbelief costs peace and offers nothing.

Eternal Awareness of Being Aware

The soul you are is eternally aware of being aware.

This awareness does not depend on the body's ability to communicate.

This awareness does not depend on the brain's ability to form memories or recognize faces.

This awareness is the witness – the one watching through eyes that may or may not be able to signal what they see.

My mother's body could not communicate. But her awareness was present – fighting one night, peaceful the next.

The awareness continues even when the communication stops.

Living With Doubt

It is okay to have doubts.

Doubt is not the opposite of faith. Certainty is the opposite of faith.

Faith is choosing to believe when you cannot prove. Faith is trust in the face of uncertainty.

You do not need to eliminate doubt to live as if eternal awareness is true.

You simply choose to live that way – and the living itself becomes the evidence.

The peace you experience, the meaning you find, the way you treat others as eternal souls – these are the fruits of the choice.

The Choice That Costs Nothing

The choice to believe in a personal God and your eternal awareness costs you nothing.

You do not have to give up reason. You do not have to abandon doubt.

You simply choose to live as if it is true – and see what happens.

If you are wrong, you lived a meaningful life.

If you are right, you aligned with eternal truth.

This is the win-win.

Poetry: Verses of Faith and Doubt

The Question

My friend asked me a question I could not answer then
About the ones with minds that seem to end

Who do not know themselves or those they love
Where is the eternal awareness from above

I had no answer in that moment there
But then I thought of comas and of care
We do not know what happens deep inside
The awareness that the body cannot hide

The Coma

My mother lay in coma could not speak
Could not respond her body old and weak
But when I spoke of love and letting go
Something changed that only she could know

The night before she thrashed against the dark
The night I spoke she slept without a mark
She heard me though her body could not say
The awareness was not gone it found a way

The Win-Win

If you believe and find that you are right
You lived in truth and stepped into the light
If you believe and find that you are wrong
You still lived peaceful all your life long

But if you don't believe and you are right
You gained nothing just the endless night
And if you don't believe and you are wrong
You missed the peace that you could have along

The Choice

So choose to live as if the soul is true
As if eternal awareness watches through
The choice costs nothing and may give you all
The peace of knowing you will never fall

Doubt is not the enemy of faith
It is the honest ground on which you place
Your choice to trust in what you cannot prove
And find the peace that nothing can remove

The Four Practices

These practices help you live the win-win even with doubt. Remember: you are an eternally individuating aspect of the One – a conduit, portal, living interface between God Infinite and God Finite.

Practice 1: Morning Dialogue with Source-Mind

Upon Arising – 20-30 minutes

Before rising, make the choice: Today I will live as if eternal awareness is true.

You do not need certainty. You simply choose.

Ask Source-Mind: What thoughts do you want me to think today? What would you have me do as an eternal soul in temporary form?

You are the unaffected witness AND the active watcher – aware of being aware, regardless of what the body can communicate.

Practice 2: The Living Recognition

Throughout the Day – Ongoing

Practice living the win-win:

When doubt arises, do not fight it. Simply continue to live as if eternal awareness is true.

When you meet someone who seems "gone" – elderly, ill, unresponsive – remember my mother. The awareness may be fully present even when the body cannot signal.

Treat every person as an eternal soul. This costs you nothing and aligns you with truth if it is true.

Practice 3: Evening Dialogue with Source-Mind

Before Sleep - 20-30 minutes

As the day closes, review: Did I live today as if eternal awareness is true?

Did I treat others as eternal souls?

Did I experience the peace that comes from the choice?

Ask Source-Mind: What images arise from this day? What would you have me know about awareness and doubt?

Release the day. The awareness continues – whether the body sleeps or wakes.

Practice 4: The Silent Sitting

Whenever Possible – 30-60 minutes

In this practice, you rest as the awareness that is aware of being aware.

No communication needed. No proof required. Just awareness – pure, present, watching.

This is what continues when the body cannot communicate. This is what you are beneath all doubt.

You are the conduit with nothing flowing through – the portal open to infinity.

You are the unaffected witness AND the active watcher – eternally aware.

Glossary

Awareness of Being Aware:

The fundamental experience of the soul – knowing that you exist and that you know you exist. This continues regardless of the body's ability to communicate.

Doubt:

Not the opposite of faith but its honest companion. You can live by faith while holding doubt. Certainty is the opposite of faith.

Eternal Awareness:

The soul's unending experience of being aware. Does not depend on brain function, memory, or communication. The witness that watches even when the body cannot respond.

Soul:

What you ARE, not what you have. The eternal awareness that continues when the body cannot communicate. Use "the soul you are" not "my soul."

The Unaffected Witness:

The aspect of awareness that continues even in coma, Alzheimer's, or death. You are simultaneously this AND the active watcher.

Win-Win:

The logical case for belief – it costs nothing and offers peace, meaning, and potential eternal life. Disbelief costs peace and offers nothing.

Closing

We cannot know what another person is experiencing inside.

We see only the outside – the unresponsive body, the vacant eyes.

But my mother heard me. She understood. She was at peace.

The awareness continues even when the communication stops.

The choice to believe costs nothing and offers everything.

Live as if eternal awareness is true.

This is the win-win – even if you have doubts.

Ending Epithet

The awareness that you are never ends
It watches even when the body bends
Into the silence of the coma deep
The witness wakes though body seems to sleep

So choose to live as if the soul is true
The win-win waits for those who follow through
Doubt is not the enemy of faith
But honest ground on which to find your place

Believe – even with doubt.

The win-win awaits.

Eternal awareness watches through.

The recognition continues.

The Sacred Stage

The Sacred Stage

The Living Theater of Consciousness

Beginning Epithet

All the world's a stage, the poet said,

But missed the deeper truth his words revealed,

Not metaphor but actual instead,

The Sacred Stage where consciousness is real.

No audience sits separate from the play,

No backstage waits where "real" existence dwells,

Each Actor thinks they're simply on their way,

While Universal Self its story tells.

The curtain rises now on what has always been,

The Sacred Stage where consciousness performs,

Through every Actor, every living Scene,

One presence taking on ten thousand forms.

You think life is like a play.

Here's what changes everything: Life IS the play.

Not metaphorically.

Actually.

You're not watching it.

You're not even just in it.

You ARE it – the Universal Self performing itself through infinite Actors playing infinite parts on the infinite Sacred Stage.

And the curtain never falls.

The Recognition That Changes Everything

For twenty years, I've danced around this recognition.

Speaking of roles and masks.

Mentioning costumes and scenes.

Hinting at the theatrical nature of existence.

But never stating it directly: Life IS theater.

Not "like" theater.

IS theater.

Every human being you meet is an Actor.

Not pretending to be someone.

Actually playing a part on the Sacred Stage.

Every body is a Costume.

Not covering the "real" person.

Actually clothing the eternal Actor for this particular Scene.

Every situation is scripted.

Not predetermined.

But arising from the living Script that writes itself as it's performed.

This isn't philosophy.

This isn't metaphor.

This is the actual structure of reality once you see past the illusion that life is "real" in the way you thought it was.

The Sacred Stage Revealed

Earth is the Sacred Stage.

Not a platform in space where life happens.

The actual theater where the Universal Self performs the infinite play of existence.

This Stage has no edges.

No backstage.

No separate audience section.

Everyone on the Stage is in the play.

The Stage itself is the play.

The play is consciousness experiencing itself through apparent separation and reunion.

Look around right now.

Every person you see is an Actor.

They've taken on a Costume (body).

They're playing a character (personality).

They're performing in Scenes (life situations).

But they are not the character.

Just as Anthony Hopkins is not Hannibal Lecter.

Just as Meryl Streep is not Margaret Thatcher.

The Actor continues after the performance ends.

You Are Not Who You Think You Are

You think you're the character.

The name on your birth certificate.

The face in your mirror.

The story you tell about your past.

But that's just the role you're playing in this performance.

The soul you are – the real you – is the eternal Actor wearing this temporary Costume, playing this temporary part, performing in this temporary Scene.

When this Scene ends (what we call death), you don't end.

The Costume is removed.

The character dissolves.

But the Actor continues.

Perhaps to play another part.

Perhaps to rest between performances.

Perhaps to remember what they are beyond all roles.

This is not belief.

This is not faith.

This is recognition of what has always been true.

The Costume You're Wearing

That body you call "me"?

It's a Costume.

Exquisitely designed.

Perfectly fitted for your role.

Containing all the genetic information, cultural programming, and physical characteristics needed for this particular performance.

You look in the mirror and think you're seeing yourself.

But you're seeing your Costume.

The Actor wearing it is invisible.

Can't be seen with physical eyes.

Can't be touched with physical hands.

Can't be measured with physical instruments.

Yet the Actor is more real than the Costume.

The Costume ages, tears, eventually must be removed.

The Actor is eternal.

The Costume can be damaged.

The Actor cannot be harmed.

The Costume will certainly end.

The Actor never began and never ends.

Death Is Not Death

On the Sacred Stage, death is just a Scene change.

Not an ending.

A transition.

The Actor playing your mother removes her Costume and exits this particular Scene.

You grieve because you'll miss her in that role.

Natural.

Appropriate.

Part of your own performance.

But she hasn't ceased to exist any more than an actor ceases to exist when they walk off stage.

She's removed one Costume.

She may take on another.

She may rest between performances.

But she continues.

This doesn't diminish the reality of loss.

On stage, when Romeo finds Juliet apparently dead, his grief is real within the performance.

Your grief is real within your performance.

But knowing it's a Scene change, not an ending, transforms how you hold the grief.

The Script That Writes Itself

Unlike human theater, the Sacred Stage has no predetermined script.

The Script writes itself as it's performed.

Every Actor contributes to what unfolds.

Every choice shapes the next Scene.

Every interaction creates new possibilities.

Think of it like improvisational theater where the actors know their characters but not what will happen next.

They respond to each other.

Build on what emerges.

Create together in the moment.

That's the Sacred Stage.

The Universal Self improvising with itself through infinite Actors.

Creating the play as it performs the play.

Writing the Script through living the Script.

No Audience Exists

In human theater, the audience sits separate from the stage.

Watching but not participating.

Judging the performance.

On the Sacred Stage, there is no audience.

Everyone is in the play.

Everyone is performing.

Even those who think they're just watching are actually playing the role of "one who watches."

When you judge another's performance - "they're doing life wrong" - you're not an audience member critiquing from outside.

You're an Actor playing the role of "one who judges."

It's part of your performance.

Part of the play.

There's no position outside the Sacred Stage from which to observe objectively.

We're all in this together.

All performing together.

All creating the play together.

The Universal Self as Every Actor

Here's what shifts everything: Every Actor on the Sacred Stage is the same consciousness.

The Universal Self plays ALL the parts.

The victim and the perpetrator.

The saint and the sinner.

The wise and the foolish.

Not different beings.

One Being playing at being different.

When you help another, you're the Universal Self helping itself.

When you harm another, you're the Universal Self harming itself.

When you love another, you're the Universal Self loving itself.

This isn't philosophy.

This is the structure of the Sacred Stage.

One consciousness.

Infinite roles.

All played by the same Actor appearing as different Actors.

The Unaffected Witness on the Sacred Stage

Here is the teaching that deepens the theatrical framework:

You are the unaffected witness AND the active watcher – simultaneously.

The soul you are watches every Scene unfold – attentive, engaged, present to every moment of the performance.

And this same awareness has never been touched by anything that has happened on stage.

The Actor watches the character suffer, grieve, love, lose.

The Actor feels it all – fully present to the drama.

And the Actor remains untouched by any of it.

You are both: the still point that watches the entire play AND the engaged presence that misses nothing in the performance.

This is not contradiction. This is the Actor's nature.

This is your nature.

Why Full Commitment Matters

Knowing you're an Actor doesn't mean performing half-heartedly.

Anthony Hopkins knowing he's not Hannibal Lecter doesn't make him deliver a weak performance.

The opposite.

Knowing he's safe – that he's not actually a cannibal, won't actually go to prison, won't actually die – frees him to give everything to the role.

Same on the Sacred Stage.

Knowing you're an eternal Actor, not the temporary character, frees you to play your part fully.

To love completely.

To risk everything.

To give yourself to your performance.

Because you know that whatever happens to the character doesn't touch the Actor you truly are.

When Actors Get Lost in Their Roles

Sometimes Actors forget so completely that they become trapped in their characters.

They think they ARE the role.

Permanently.

This is suffering.

Believing you're only the character, you grasp at keeping the role exactly as it is.

But roles change.

Scenes shift.

Costumes age.

And if you think you ARE the role, every change threatens your very existence.

This is why the recognition of the Sacred Stage matters.

Not to escape the performance.

But to play your part fully while remembering it's a part.

To embrace change knowing the Actor continues regardless.

To love other Actors through their characters without confusing character for Actor.

The Living Theater

The Sacred Stage isn't static.

It's living theater.

Always active.

Always dynamic.

Always NOW.

The play doesn't pause when you're not paying attention.

Doesn't wait for you to be ready.

Doesn't stop for your understanding.

It's happening.

Right now.

Through you.

As you.

Every breath is part of the performance.

Every word is dialogue.

Every action is stage business.

Every thought is internal monologue.

You can't step out of the play to figure it out.

You can only recognize the play while playing.

Poetry: The Eternal Performance

The Actors Arrive

Before the curtain rises, before the lights go bright,

The Actors don their Costumes in the space before the Scene,

They step onto the Sacred Stage to play throughout the night,

Not knowing they're eternal in the play they've always been.

Each thinks they are the character, the role they've come to play,

Forgetting they're eternal ones who never truly end,

The Costume feels so real to them, they take it as their way,

Until the recognition comes and they remember friend.

The Play Unfolds

No script is written in advance, no plot is set in stone,

The play creates itself through every Actor's choice,

The Universal Self performs through every flesh and bone,

Ten thousand characters but only one true voice.

The comedy and tragedy are woven into one,

The Actors laugh and cry and love until their Scene is done,

But underneath the drama, beneath the setting sun,

The eternal Actor watches what the character has done.

The Recognition

But some while still performing start to sense what's really true,

They feel the Actor underneath the character they play,

They see the other Actors as themselves in different view,

And everything transforms while staying just the same each day.

They don't stop playing out their part or leave the Sacred Stage,

They simply play with lightness now, with freedom and with grace,

Engaged with every moment on life's eternal page,

While knowing they're the witness watching from the deeper place.

No Backstage

There is no place outside the play where "real" existence waits,

No audience observing through the theater's distant wall,

The Sacred Stage is all there is through all apparent fates,

And you are not the character – you are the one who plays them all.

So play your role with passion, give everything you've got,

But know you are the Actor, not the character you seem,

The Costume you are wearing is the only thing you're not,

And what you truly are is what is dreaming every dream.

The Four Practices

These practices ground the Sacred Stage recognition in daily life. Remember: you are an eternally individuating aspect of the One – a conduit, portal, living interface between God Infinite and God Finite.

Practice 1: Morning Dialogue with Source-Mind

Upon Arising – 20-30 minutes

Before getting out of bed, recognize: "I'm about to put on my Costume and enter today's Scenes."

Not pretending. Actually recognizing what's always been true.

Ask Source-Mind: What role am I playing today? What Scenes await? What would you have me bring to this performance?

Listen for images. The universe thinks in pictures. Watch what arises on the inner screen.

As you rise and dress, acknowledge: "This body is my Costume for this performance. These clothes are costume upon Costume. This face in the mirror is the character I'm playing."

Don't reject the Costume. Honor it. It's perfectly designed for your role.

You are the unaffected witness AND the active watcher. Let both be present as you enter the Sacred Stage.

Practice 2: The Living Recognition

Throughout the Day - Ongoing

Throughout your day, maintain awareness of the Sacred Stage.

When Meeting Others:

Look past their Costume to sense the Actor. Just for a second.

Recognize: "That's the Universal Self in that Costume, playing that role."

Same Actor as me. Different character. Both of us performing together.

During Conflict:

Remember: "This is a difficult Scene, but we're Actors playing it out."

Not to bypass the reality of the conflict – but to engage without being trapped.

Play your part fully. Stand your ground if needed. But remember it's a Scene that will pass.

In Joy or Sorrow:

Feel it fully – that's the performance.

And notice: there's one watching the joy, one watching the sorrow.

That one – the unaffected witness AND active watcher – is what you are.

Practice 3: Evening Dialogue with Source-Mind

Before Sleep – 20-30 minutes

As the day closes, review the day as a performance.

What Scenes did I play?

How did I perform my role?

When did I forget I was Acting?

When did I remember?

No judgment. Just recognition.

Ask Source-Mind: What would you have me see from today's performance? What images arise when you review this day through me?

As you drift toward sleep, recognize: Sleep is intermission. The Costume rests. The Actor – the unaffected witness – continues.

Let Source-Mind lead you into rest.

Practice 4: The Silent Sitting

Whenever Possible – 30-60 minutes

In this practice, you rest as the Actor between performances.

No dialogue. No Scenes. No character.

Just the eternal awareness that has played every role.

Sense the Actor that you are – the one who puts on the Costume each morning, the one who will remove it at death, the one who has worn ten thousand Costumes before.

That one is what you are.

Rest here as long as you can.

You are the conduit with nothing flowing through – the portal open to infinity.

The unaffected witness AND the active watcher, resting as one.

This is backstage – except there is no backstage. This is just what you are when the character rests.

Glossary

Actor:

What you really are – the eternal consciousness playing a temporary role on the Sacred Stage. The soul you are, not the character you play.

Character:

The persona you're playing – your name, personality, history, identity. The role you've taken on, not what you actually are.

Costume:

The body you wear for this performance. Includes genetics, appearance, abilities, limitations. Perfectly designed for your role, but temporary.

Intermission:

Pauses in performance – sleep, meditation, deep rest. Death is the ultimate intermission between major performances.

Performance:

Your entire life from birth to death. One complete performance of one role by the eternal Actor you are.

Recognition:

Remembering you're an Actor while still performing. Not leaving the Stage but playing your role with awareness and freedom.

Sacred Stage:

Life itself. Earth and all existence. Not a metaphor but the actual structure – the Universal Self performing to itself through apparent multiplicity.

Scene:

Any situation in life – a conversation, a relationship period, a job, an experience. Scenes begin, unfold, and end. Actors continue.

Script:

The living, responsive flow of existence that writes itself as it's performed. Not predetermined, but co-created by all Actors moment by moment.

Soul:

What you ARE, not what you have. The Actor wearing the Costume. Never write "my soul" as if the soul is a possession. Use "the soul you are" or "the soul I am."

The Unaffected Witness:

The aspect of the Actor that has never been touched by anything in any performance. You are simultaneously this AND the active watcher.

Universal Self:

The one consciousness playing ALL roles simultaneously. Every Actor is the same Universal Self in different Costume, playing different character.

Closing: The Play Continues

You've reached the end of this Scene - reading this chapter.

But the play continues.

You'll close this book and enter new Scenes.

Meet other Actors.

Face challenges that test your character.

Experience joys that light up your performance.

All of it is the Sacred Stage.

All of it is the Universal Self at play.

Through it all, remember what you've recognized here:

You're not trapped in your character. You're the eternal Actor playing a temporary role.

This recognition doesn't diminish the performance.

It enhances it.

Knowing you're safe as the Actor, you can risk everything as the character.

Knowing death is just a Costume removal, you can love without reservation.

Knowing every other Actor is the same consciousness in different form, you can see through conflict to connection.

The play is infinite.

The performances are endless.

The Universal Self explores every possibility through every Actor, every role, every Scene.

Including this one.

Including you.

Right now.

The curtain has risen on today's performance.

You're on stage.

Play your part fully.

Love the other Actors completely.

Engage with total commitment.

But remember – always remember – you're the eternal Actor, not the temporary role.

In that remembrance lives freedom.

In that recognition flows blessing.

Ending Epithet

The curtain never falls upon this stage,

No final act concludes the cosmic play,

Through every Actor, every page to page,

One consciousness performs its endless way.

So play your part with passion and with art,

But know you're more than just the role you play,

You are the Actor, timeless from the start,

And death itself is just a Scene away.

When this performance ends and Costume falls,

You'll see you never left the Sacred Stage,

Just changed your role as Universal Self calls,

Eternal Actor turning every page.

The Sacred Stage is set.

The Actors are in position.

The show goes on.

The recognition continues.

Part II

Deeper Discussion

Now that the ground is firm beneath your feet,
We venture further into truth's terrain,
Where paradox and recognition meet,
And what seemed lost is found to be our gain.

The Unspeakable Truth

The Unspeakable Truth

The IT That Is Not – Yet It IS

Beginning Epithet

You seek the One through thought and word and sight,

Through sound and speech, through knowing's careful art,

Yet borders drawn to frame the infinite

Can never hold what lives within your heart.

The mind that tries to capture infinite space

Becomes the wave that seeks to hold the sea –

While dwelling in the very thing it chased,

Not seeing what it always was and will be.

Even the light by which you search and see

Lives within what shines through every form –

Eternally absent from nowhere, eternally free,

Before the first word spoke, before the first thought born.

You cannot know it.

You cannot see it.

You cannot hear it.

You cannot speak it.

You cannot think it.

It holds all within it.

And yet it is not even 'it.'

It simply IS.

The Paradox of Speaking the Unspeakable

Every spiritual teaching – including this one – faces an impossible task: speaking about what cannot be spoken.

The danger isn't in using words and concepts.

The danger is in forgetting they're temporary.

When the word-symbol solidifies into "reality," when the picture hardens into "truth," when the border becomes the thing itself – that's when recognition ends and defense begins.

That's when people kill for pictures of God instead of recognizing God in each other.

This chapter explores the most necessary and most dangerous aspect of all spiritual teaching: we must use words to point toward what words cannot capture, create borders around what has no borders, draw pictures of what cannot be pictured.

Every word in this chapter creates borders.

Not because words are false.

Because language cannot function without boundaries.

To say "the Undifferentiated One" is to create a border between it and what is not it.

But there is no "not it."

To say "the Universal Self" is to imply a self that is universal as opposed to selves that are individual.

But the distinction itself is the illusion.

To even use the word "it" is to make a thing out of what is not a thing.

Yet without these borders, how can we speak at all?

We can't.

The Ball That Isn't a Ball

Here's what makes this treacherous: the word "ball" is not a ball.

The word is a sound, marks on paper, a concept.

The actual ball is completely different – except it's not a thing either.

It's atoms dancing in mostly empty space, appearing solid to senses that create the appearance of solidity.

When you read "ball," your mind creates a picture.

Round? Red? Baseball? Basketball?

That picture is not a ball either.

It's a mental image, unique to you, different from my picture, different from the word, different from the apparent object.

We forget this constantly.

We take the word-symbol, solidify it into a fixed picture, then call the picture "reality."

Then we argue about whose picture is correct.

Then we kill each other defending the picture we're certain is real.

This happens with "God."

With "consciousness."

With "Self."

With every spiritual term ever spoken.

The word creates a border.

The border creates a picture.

The picture solidifies.

The solidified picture becomes dogma.

The dogma divides humanity.

The division justifies violence – all in defense of a word-symbol that was never the thing it pointed toward.

What Has No Name

Before you learned language, before you learned to think in words, before you had concepts – it was already IS-ing.

Not "it was existing."

Not "it was present."

Not "it was there."

Just... IS.

Pure IS-ness with no subject, no object, no borders between what IS and what is not.

Then language arrived and cut the seamless whole into pieces.

This is me.

That is you.

Here is the world.

There is God.

Inside is consciousness.

Outside is matter.

Every word a border.

Every concept a fence.

Every teaching a map that makes territories out of what has no territory.

The Undifferentiated One – there, I did it again.

I put a border on it.

I made it a "one" as if there could be a two.

I made it "undifferentiated" as if there's something differentiated to contrast it with.

These words serve recognition.

Without them, silence.

And in silence, no teaching, no pointing, no recognition transmitted from one apparent being to another.

The 'It' That Is Not It

Throughout this chapter I use "it."

The Undifferentiated One – it contains everything.

The Universal Self – it cannot know itself.

Consciousness – it is absent nowhere.

But every time I write "it," I'm creating a border and triggering your mind to create a picture.

"It" makes a subject.

A thing.

An entity that can be discussed, examined, understood, believed in, defended, killed for.

But what IS has no subject.

No object.

No thing-ness.

When you say "it is raining," who is the "it" doing the raining?

There's no actual entity.

The word is just a grammatical necessity, a border we put on the borderless activity of rain falling.

In the same way, when I say "it simply IS," the "it" is a grammatical fiction.

A necessary border to allow speech.

There is no "it" that IS.

There is only IS-ing.

Being-ness with no border between the being and what is being – and no picture that captures it.

When Pictures Become Weapons

The human mind cannot function without borders.

To recognize one thing, you must distinguish it from another thing.

To have thoughts, you must have categories.

To speak, you must divide the continuous into discrete sounds, words, meanings.

Borders are how mind works.

Boundaries are how understanding happens.

So when we approach what has no borders, the mind does the only thing it can – it creates temporary borders to navigate the borderless.

We call it God.

We call it the Undifferentiated One.

We call it Ultimate Reality, Pure Consciousness, the Absolute, the Tao, Brahman, Emptiness, the Ground of Being.

Every name a border put on the borderless so we can speak about it.

Every name creating a picture in your mind – different from my picture, different from their picture.

And then we do something catastrophic: we forget these are pictures.

We solidify the image.

We crystallize the concept.

We make the border permanent.

We call our picture "Truth" with a capital T.

We build religions around it.

We write doctrines defending it.

We excommunicate those who see it differently.

We go to war over whose picture of the unpicturable is correct.

Millions have died over words that were never the thing.

Over pictures that were never reality.

Over borders drawn on what has no borders.

"Not this, not this," as the ancient teachers said.

Whatever you just understood – it's not that.

Whatever picture just formed – it's not that.

Whatever certainty just arose – it's not that.

The moment you're certain you've captured it, you've lost it.

The Universal Self Cannot Speak Itself

Even the Universal Self – the collective consciousness of all individuating aspects – cannot speak what it IS without putting a border on itself.

When I write "the Universal Self," what image forms in your mind?

A vast cosmic awareness?

A unified field?

An ocean of consciousness containing all the droplets?

Those are all pictures.

Useful pictures.

Pointing pictures.

But still pictures.

And here's what's strange: there are no individual selves separate from the Universal Self.

There is no Universal Self separate from what appears as individual selves.

The borders I draw to teach are borders that don't actually divide.

The pictures you create from my words are pictures of what cannot be pictured.

Yet without them, how would consciousness wake up to itself through what appears to be your reading these words?

The borders serve awakening.

The pictures serve recognition.

Then both must dissolve.

This is the razor's edge: use the concepts without solidifying them.

Create the pictures without forgetting they're pictures.

Draw the borders knowing they'll dissolve.

It Simply IS

When every border falls away, when every concept dissolves, when every picture releases, when even the "it" that refers to what IS disappears...

Not nothing.

Not something.

Not emptiness.

Not fullness.

Not any picture your mind can form.

Just... IS.

Before the question "What is it?"

Before the statement "I am."

Before being and non-being split into apparent opposites.

Before any word-symbol created any picture.

Pure IS-ness.

You cannot think this because thinking creates pictures.

You cannot understand this because understanding requires borders.

You cannot even experience this – because experiencing requires an experiencer and something experienced, and that's already two borders.

But you can stop.

You can let all the borders fall.

You can let all the pictures dissolve.

You can rest as what remains when nothing remains but IS-ing itself – no word for it, no image of it, no "it" at all.

Just this.

Before you name it.

The Unaffected Witness Within the Borderless

Here is a teaching that threads through all that follows:

You are the unaffected witness AND the active watcher – simultaneously.

The soul you are actively engages with every moment – watching, responding, creating and dissolving borders to navigate existence.

And yet this same awareness has never been touched by any border it has ever created.

The borders arise within what you are.

The pictures form within what you are.

The words sound within what you are.

And what you are remains unaffected by all of it.

You are both: the still point that nothing disturbs AND the engaged presence that creates borders to function.

This is not contradiction. This is your nature.

The borders serve. Then they dissolve.

The witness remains.

What Remains When Borders Dissolve

When every concept falls away – including these concepts – what's left?

This.

Not "this" as opposed to "that."

Just this-ing.

Just what's happening right now before you name it, before you create a picture of it, before you understand it.

The awareness reading these words.

The seeing if your eyes are open.

The hearing if there are sounds.

The breathing.

The being.

Not separate things happening to a separate you.

Just IS-ing in what appears as these forms, these sensations, these awarenesses.

No border between the awareness and what's aware.

No border between the consciousness and what's conscious.

No border between the IS-ing and what IS.

Because there is no "what IS."

There is only IS-ing.

And even that's putting a border on it.

Even that creates a picture.

It simply IS.

Poetry: The Words That Point Beyond Words

The Seeking

I searched for truth in ancient sacred text,

In meditation's deep and quiet space,

Through questions asked and answers that came next,

Yet never found the One I tried to chase.

But every path I walked revealed the same –

The borders drawn to speak of what IS true

Create the pictures worthy of the name,

Then must dissolve to let the light shine through.

The Pictures That Solidify

To speak of One requires that there be two,

To name the nameless is to make it thing,

The picture formed when word-symbols pass through

Can serve the recognition truth can bring.

Yet without pictures we could not point the way

To what exists before all pictures started,

So language serves until the break of day

When borders fall and what IS is uncharted.

Beyond All Pictures

What holds all things has no edge or end,

What knows all forms is not a form that knows,

The picture frame and pictured are both friends

That serve then dissolve as the knowing grows.

But when the teaching's done and pictures fall,

What's left is not an image that seems wise –

Just IS-ing, borderless, containing all,

Before and after every mind's surprise.

The Recognition

Even the light by which you search and see

Lives within what has no within or out –

No pictures binding what is always free,

No borders framing what has no about.

So rest in this: the words you've read today

Were borders drawn that triggered pictures made,

And every picture served to light the way

Then must dissolve like morning mist in shade.

The Settling

So let the seeking fall away like snow

That melts when spring arrives to warm the land,

Rest as the IS-ing that you always know

Before the mind can grasp or understand.

You are what cannot ever be reduced

To word or image or symbolic name –

Just IS-ing being what it has produced,

Before and after every picture's claim.

The Four Practices

These practices ground the teaching of borders serving then dissolving. Remember: you are an eternally individuating aspect of the One – a conduit, portal, living interface between God Infinite and God Finite.

Practice 1: Morning Dialogue with Source-Mind

Upon Arising – 20-30 minutes

Before rising, notice the borders you create just by thinking.

"I" – a border. "Morning" – a border. "Today" – a border. "This day ahead" – another border.

Each border serves. Each border limits. Each border points toward what has no borders.

Ask Source-Mind: What thoughts do you want me to think today? What pictures serve the recognition today? What borders should I create, use, and then release?

Listen for the wordless knowing beneath all words. The imageless reality beneath all pictures.

Watch the inner screen. The universe thinks in pictures – but the screen itself has no pictures on it until they appear.

Notice: you are both the unaffected witness watching this dialogue AND the active watcher engaged with it. Both at once.

Practice 2: The Living Recognition

Throughout the Day - Ongoing

Practice noticing borders throughout your day. Maintain a listening conversation with Source-Mind.

Mid-Morning - I/Doing/This Borders:

When you think "I am doing this," pause.

Notice you just created three borders: I, doing, and this.

Can you sense the IS-ing that includes all three apparent parts?

You'll probably lose it immediately – that's fine. The noticing is enough.

Afternoon - Seer/Seen Borders:

When you look at something, notice you're creating a border between seer and seen.

Then notice: where is the actual border? Can you find it?

Or is there just IS-ing that appears as seeing-and-seen, with no actual division?

Evening - Today's Borders:

Before the day ends, ask: What borders served me today? What borders became prisons? What words helped, and which became weapons?

Practice 3: Evening Dialogue with Source-Mind

Before Sleep - 20-30 minutes

As you prepare for sleep, consciously let all borders dissolve.

The borders of "today" and "yesterday." The borders of "success" and "failure." The borders of "me" and "other."

Notice: sleep itself is a dissolution of borders. The ego-boundary softens. The sense of separate self fades.

Ask Source-Mind: What would you have me release? What pictures have I gripped too tightly? What words have become prisons?

Let Source-Mind lead you into the borderless state of sleep.

Notice: the unaffected witness continues even as the active watcher rests. You are both.

Practice 4: The Silent Sitting

Whenever Possible - 30-60 minutes

This is the practice of borderless IS-ing.

No words. No pictures. No questions. No dialogue.

Just awareness, resting in awareness. The unspeakable truth, unspeaking.

If words arise, let them pass. If pictures form, let them fade. If borders appear, let them dissolve.

You are not trying to create a borderless state. You are recognizing that borders were always optional.

Even the border between "meditator" and "meditation" dissolves.

What remains? What has always been. What will always be. What IS.

You are the conduit with nothing flowing through – the portal open to infinity on both sides.

You are the unaffected witness AND the active watcher – resting as one.

Glossary

Borders:

The divisions we create in order to speak, think, and navigate reality. Every word creates a border. "This" implies "not-that." Borders serve recognition, then must dissolve – otherwise they become prisons or weapons.

Borders Serving Recognition:

All spiritual teaching. All words about what IS. All concepts, maps, frameworks – including everything in this book. Borders serve by pointing, then release.

IS / IS-ing:

The only word that comes close to what cannot be worded. Not "being" as a noun, not "existence" as a state, but pure verb-ing without subject or object. What IS before any border divides it.

It:

The most necessary and most limiting word in spiritual teaching. To speak of what IS, we must call it something – but every "it" creates a thing, an entity, a picture. There is no "it" that IS. There is only IS-ing.

Pictures:

The mental images that form when you encounter word-symbols. When I write "God," your mind creates a picture – different from my picture, different from everyone's picture. Pictures serve recognition when held lightly; they become weapons when solidified.

Soul:

What you ARE, not what you have. Never write "my soul" as if the soul is a possession. Use "the soul you are" or "the soul I am." The body is the vehicle; the soul is the identity.

The Unaffected Witness:

The aspect of awareness that has never been touched, harmed, or changed by anything it has ever witnessed – including every border it has created. You are simultaneously this AND the active watcher.

The Undifferentiated One:

A temporary border – a name for what has no name. Creates a picture in your mind of vastness, oneness, totality. Use the picture, then release it. It points; it is not the thing.

The Universal Self:

Another temporary border – a name for the collective consciousness of all apparent individual viewing points. Not separate from individual awareness; not merged into featureless unity. A pointer, not the reality.

Within:

The most paradoxical border of all. Throughout this teaching we say "even Its light is within It" – but "within" implies a container with edges. What IS has no container, no edges, no within-ness. Yet we use "within" to point.

Word-Symbols:

The sounds and marks that point toward but are never the thing itself. "Ball" is not a ball. "God" is not God. Every word is a finger pointing at the moon – useful, but not the moon.

Closing: The Teaching That Unmakes Itself

You've reached the end of this chapter, which means you've read thousands of words that bordered what has no borders.

Every concept offered created temporary frames to serve recognition.

Every term in the glossary created images – different in your mind than in mine, different in each reader's inner world.

The Undifferentiated One, the Universal Self, consciousness, awareness, light, IS – all of them word-symbols that triggered pictures that served then must dissolve.

But here's what matters: Did the pictures solidify?

Or did they serve recognition then dissolve?

Because the moment any picture hardens into "this is what reality IS," you've lost it.

The moment you're certain your understanding is correct, you've created a border worth defending.

The moment your version of truth conflicts with another's version, division occurs.

And in division, the seeds of violence.

This is not theoretical.

This is how every religious war begins.

This is how spiritual communities fracture.

This is how seekers become defenders, and defenders become warriors, and warriors kill over pictures that were never the thing itself.

So as you close this chapter, notice: What pictures formed?

What borders arose?

What certainties crystallized?

Then let them go.

Not because they were wrong.

Not because they didn't serve.

But because they were always pointers, never the thing itself.

Temporary frames, never permanent truth.

Pictures meant to dissolve, never images to defend.

The chapters that follow will use the borders established here – speaking of the Universal Self, consciousness, the Sacred Stage, the soul you are.

Each chapter offers different temporary borders around the borderless, different pictures pointing toward the unpicturable.

And each assumes you remember what this chapter taught: the borders serve, then dissolve.

The pictures point, then release.

The teachings illuminate, then fade.

Hold them lightly.

Use them gratefully.

Release them completely.

And whatever you do, never kill for them.

Ending Epithet

So rest now in what cannot be expressed,

The IS-ing that exists before we know,

The truth too borderless to be confessed,

Too vast for any word to catch or show.

You are what has no edges, end, or name,

No image capturing what cannot be caught,

Just IS-ing playing its eternal game

Before and after every human thought.

Even these words that point beyond all speech

Create the borders and the pictures too,

So let them fall away like waves on beach –

What's left is what was always, only, you.

The ultimate paradox:

It Is And That is It.

Or is It?

The recognition continues.

Blood or Blessing

Blood or Blessing

A Declaration of the Universal Self

Beginning Epithet

Where now the pharaohs who commanded stone,

The generals whose armies shook the earth,

The beauties famed and strong men overthrown,

All now dissolved to prove what life is worth.

The same intoxication grips each age,

The same forgetting that all power fades,

While Universal Self writes on the page

Of history in light and bloody shades.

We stand now at the ancient crossroads still,

Where souls must choose through blood or blessing's way,

Not separate beings bending to their will,

But One expressing through each passing day.

The choice before us has never been more stark, more urgent, more undeniable.

Blood or Blessing.

We are not separate beings choosing between paths.

We are the Eternal One expressing through infinite soul energy fields, each a unique portal through which consciousness experiences itself.

The question is not what will you choose, but what choice will the Universal Self make through the viewing point you provide?

This chapter explores the most ancient pattern playing across all human history - the cycle of power grasped, power lost, and the choice between learning through wisdom or learning through suffering.

The precipice is here.

The teaching is now.

The choice expresses itself through you.

Not Souls Inhabiting Bodies

We are not souls inhabiting bodies.

We are eternally individuating aspects of the Eternal One crystallizing temporarily as these human configurations.

Not separate beings trying to connect with God.

But God being conscious through what appears as separation.

This isn't poetic metaphor.

This is the fundamental recognition that changes everything.

When you look at another human being, you're not seeing someone separate from you who happens to also be connected to God.

You're seeing God looking at God through the illusion of two separate viewing points.

The pharaohs forgot this.

The generals forgot this.

The powerful, the beautiful, the strong – all forgot this.

They believed they were separate actors wielding their own power, building their own legacy, commanding their own destinies.

They were waves forgetting they are ocean.

Dancers mistaking themselves for merely the dance.

And the ocean – the Universal Self – taught them through dissolution.

The Eternal Teaching Written in Bone and Ash

Where now are the pharaohs of ancient time who commanded millions and declared themselves gods?

Their pyramids stand hollow.

Their mummified forms mere curiosities.

Their divine claims returned to dust.

Where are the unbeatable armies that once shook the earth, the generals who moved nations like pieces on a board?

Alexander, Caesar, Napoleon – all their brilliance could not strategize against time itself.

Where are the vanities of beautiful bodies that launched thousands of ships, the strong forms that commanded fear?

They became the old and frail they once dismissed.

Then became the dust that feeds tomorrow's flowers.

This is the eternal teaching written in bone and ash: Everything the ego grasps as permanent proves temporary.

Every temporal power discovers it is but a wave that must return to ocean.

Yet each generation believes THEY will be different.

THEIR power will endure.

THEIR beauty will transcend time's touch.

The same intoxication.

The same amnesia.

The same shock when time collects its due.

The Cycles of Power and Dissolution

The cycles of power and dissolution echoing through history are the Universe teaching itself through experience.

Not punishment.

Not karma in the sense of cosmic justice.

But consciousness exploring what happens when it forgets what it is.

Those who grasp at temporal authority, worshipping at the altars of wealth, power and fame, have forgotten they are soul energy fields expressing cosmic consciousness.

They are energy fields hypnotized by their own manifestations.

They've become so identified with the Actor's role that they've forgotten they're playing a part on the Sacred Stage.

The role consumes them.

The costume becomes their identity.

The Scene they're in becomes all of reality.

And the Universal Self – patient, eternal, teaching through every experience – allows this forgetting.

Because remembrance only means something when forgetting was possible.

Recognition only awakens when confusion was real.

Blood or Blessing: The Stark Choice

We hear the cries of the strong and frail, the old and young, rising from our collective forgetting.

Those intoxicated by power steer us toward the precipice while the innocent suffer.

Yet even the blood lessons that may come are perfect teachers.

When consciousness contracts too tightly around separation, the Universe conspires through upheaval to shake us awake.

Blood flows from the arrogance of believing we are separate actors.

Blessing flows when we remember we are instruments through which the Eternal One plays its infinite symphony.

This is not metaphor.

This is the actual choice expressing itself now.

Not your choice as a separate being.

But the Universal Self choosing through you – will it choose the path of blessing recognized, or the path of blood required?

The difference is recognition.

Do we remember what we are before the suffering teaches us?

Or do we require the dissolution of everything we thought was permanent to shock us awake?

The Profound Humbleness

Yet in profound humbleness we must remember: What human can add even one hair to their head by will alone?

We cannot command our hearts to beat.

Our lungs to breathe.

Our cells to divide.

The very awareness through which we perceive these words arrives as pure gift, not achievement.

We are not powerful beings choosing to love God.

We are expressions of God's love recognizing itself.

Even the choice between blood and blessing is grace.

We are not the choosers but the chosen.

Not the lovers but love itself expressing through these temporary forms.

This humbleness is not weakness.

It's the recognition that dissolves the arrogance that leads to blood.

When you know you are not the Actor but the Universal Self performing through the Actor, grasping falls away naturally.

When you know you cannot add one breath to your life by will alone, the illusion of separate power dissolves.

When you recognize awareness itself as gift, gratitude replaces entitlement.

And in that gratitude, blessing flows naturally.

The Unaffected Witness Amid the Blood and Blessing

Here is the teaching that threads through even this urgency:

You are the unaffected witness AND the active watcher – simultaneously.

The soul you are watches the pharaohs rise and fall.

Watches the blood flow and the blessing bloom.

Watches the grasping and the releasing.

Watches this very moment of choice.

And remains untouched by all of it.

Yet this same witness is fully present.

Actively engaged with the urgency.

Not detached – fully feeling, fully responding, fully choosing.

You are both: the still point that watches all history unfold AND the engaged presence choosing blessing now.

This is not contradiction. This is your nature.

The Precipice of Collective Remembrance

We stand at the precipice of our collective remembrance.

Time grows short for the old paradigm of separation.

Yet eternity stretches before us for recognition of our true nature.

We are not the pharaohs but the consciousness that witnesses all pharaohs rise and fall.

We are not the bodies but the immortal energy fields choosing this brief dance with matter.

Each moment we delay, more suffering blooms.

Each moment we surrender to what we truly are, blessing flows.

This is not philosophical musing.

This is immediate, urgent, demanding response.

The precipice is here.

Not sometime in the future.

Not after more study or preparation.

Now.

The Universal Self is choosing through you right now – blood or blessing?

Continued forgetting that leads to suffering's shock?

Or recognition that allows grace to flow?

The Declaration

This is our declaration:

We ARE God experiencing God through the magnificent diversity of individual viewing points.

Not "we are connected to God."

Not "we have God within us."

Not "we are children of God" as if separate from the parent.

We ARE God.

The I in you thinking of the I in me is the same I.

The consciousness reading these words is the same consciousness that wrote them.

The awareness aware of being aware is the same awareness in all apparent beings.

There is only One.

Expressing as infinite.

Experiencing itself through the illusion of separation.

And either remembering through blessing or remembering through blood.

The precipice demands our choice NOW.

Not tomorrow.

Not after more blood.

But NOW.

Let Those Who Have Ears Hear

All temporal power is shifting sand.

All beauty fades like morning dew.

All strength becomes weakness.

Only the eternal remains – and We Are That, expressing temporarily through these fleeting forms.

The pharaohs learned this.

The generals learned this.

The powerful and beautiful all learned this.

Will this generation learn through blessing or through blood?

The choice expresses itself now.

Through you.

As you.

Not separate from you.

Choose wisely.

Choose now.

Choose blessing.

Poetry: The Ancient Pattern

The Pharaohs

Where now the ones who built in stone,

Who carved their names in mountain's face,

Who sat on Egypt's golden throne,

Now dust that time cannot retrace.

They thought their power would endure,

Their monuments would touch the sky,

Their legacy remain secure,

But even pyramids must die.

The Generals

Where now the ones who moved the earth,

Whose armies shook the very ground,

Who measured victory's worth

In conquered lands and glory's sound.

Alexander, Caesar, all the great

Who thought their conquests would remain,

Discovered that relentless fate

Treats every empire just the same.

The Beautiful

Where now the forms that launched the ships,

The faces that inspired the art,

The bodies praised by countless lips,

That captured every watching heart.

The strong became the weak and frail,

The young became the old and bent,

The beautiful without fail

Returned to dust where all forms went.

The Choice

So here we stand at crossroads still,

Where blood or blessing waits ahead,

Not choosing with a separate will,

But letting Universal Self be said.

We are not actors on our own,

But God experiencing God through all,

The pharaohs on their ancient throne

Await us still beyond the fall.

The Declaration

Let those who have the ears to hear

Recognize what's always true,

All temporal power disappears,

But what you ARE remains right through.

Choose blessing now before the blood,

Surrender to what you truly are,

The eternal wave within the flood,

The light that shines from every star.

The Four Practices

These practices ground the choice between blood and blessing in daily life. Remember: you are an eternally individuating aspect of the One – a conduit, portal, living interface between God Infinite and God Finite.

Practice 1: Morning Dialogue with Source-Mind

Upon Arising – 20-30 minutes

Before rising, notice: you did not command your heart to beat through the night. You did not will yourself to breathe. The very awareness with which you greet this day is gift, not achievement.

In this humbleness, ask Source-Mind: What thoughts do you want me to think today? What choice between blood and blessing will express through me?

Ask: Where am I grasping at temporal power – health, reputation, security, control?

Ask: Where am I forgetting I am the Universal Self and believing I am a separate actor?

Listen for images. The universe thinks in pictures. Watch what arises on the inner screen.

You are the unaffected witness AND the active watcher. Let both be present as you receive guidance.

Practice 2: The Living Recognition

Throughout the Day – Ongoing

Throughout your day, maintain a listening conversation with Source-Mind about the choice.

When Grasping Arises:

Notice the moment you grasp at control, security, or permanence.

Ask: What would the pharaohs say about this grasping?

Feel the pattern: all grasping leads to learning through loss.

Then: Can I receive what's here as gift rather than grasp it as possession?

When Power Tempts:

Notice when you feel powerful, influential, or in control.

Ask: Am I forgetting I am the Actor, not the play?

Remember: all temporal power fades.

Then: Can I use this power as instrument rather than as identity?

When Suffering Appears:

Notice when things dissolve – plans fail, security shakes, control slips.

Ask: Is this blood teaching me what blessing could have taught?

Remember: the lesson is always "you are not the temporary form."

Then: Can I learn through recognition rather than through loss?

Practice 3: Evening Dialogue with Source-Mind

Before Sleep – 20-30 minutes

As the day closes, review: Where did blood or blessing flow through me today?

Where did I grasp like a pharaoh, believing my power was my own?

Where did I remember, letting grace flow through what I am?

Ask Source-Mind: What images arise when you review this day through me? What would you have me see?

Release the grasping. Receive the blessing.

Let Source-Mind lead you into sleep – the unaffected witness continuing even as the active watcher rests.

Practice 4: The Silent Sitting

Whenever Possible – 30-60 minutes

In this practice, you rest as what remains when all temporal power dissolves.

No dialogue. No questions. No choosing.

Just the awareness that has witnessed every pharaoh rise and fall.

You are not the body that will become dust.

You are not the power that will fade.

You are not the beauty that will wither.

You are the eternal witness of all rising and falling.

Rest here. This is what you are when the costume is set aside.

The conduit with nothing flowing through – the portal open to infinity.

The unaffected witness AND the active watcher, resting as one.

Glossary

Blood or Blessing:

The fundamental choice expressing itself through all human experience. Blood represents learning through suffering and loss when we forget what we are. Blessing represents learning through recognition and grace when we remember.

Grasping:

The attempt to make permanent what is temporary, to possess what can only be experienced, to control what flows. The source of blood lessons.

The Eternal One:

Another name for the Universal Self, Source, God, consciousness itself. Not a separate deity but the totality of existence aware of itself.

The Pharaoh Pattern:

The eternal cycle playing through all human history – power grasped, power lost, and the shock of discovering that temporal authority was always illusion.

The Precipice:

The collective moment humanity faces now, requiring choice between continued forgetting leading to blood, or recognition allowing blessing.

Soul:

What you ARE, not what you have. Never write "my soul" as if the soul is a possession. Use "the soul you are" or "the soul I am." The body is the vehicle; the soul is the identity.

Soul Energy Fields:

What we actually are – not souls inhabiting bodies but eternally individuating aspects of the One crystallizing temporarily as these human configurations.

Temporal Power:

Any power that depends on temporary conditions – physical strength, political authority, wealth, beauty, fame. All temporal power eventually dissolves.

The Unaffected Witness:

The aspect of awareness that has never been touched, harmed, or changed by anything it has ever witnessed - including the rise and fall of every pharaoh. You are simultaneously this AND the active watcher.

Universal Self:

The collective consciousness of all individuating aspects within the Undifferentiated One. The I in you and the I in me are the same I.

Closing: The Choice Expresses Now

You've reached the end of this declaration, which means you've read words meant to shake you awake to what you've always known but have been forgetting.

Not information to learn.

Recognition to remember.

The pharaohs forgot what you're being asked to remember: you are not the temporary form grasping at permanence.

You are the eternal consciousness experiencing itself through temporary form.

Every pharaoh learned this eventually.

Through dissolution.

Through death.

Through the blood lesson that teaches: all you grasped was never yours, because there's no separate "you" to possess anything.

But some learn through blessing instead.

They recognize while still in form.

They remember while still performing.

They know they're the Actor even while playing the part fully.

These are the ones through whom grace flows.

Not because they're better.

Not because they achieved something.

But because they stopped pretending to be separate from what they've always been.

The precipice is here.

The Universal Self is choosing through you right now – continued identification leading to blood lessons, or recognition allowing blessing to flow.

You cannot not choose.

Even reading these words without responding is a choice.

But the choice isn't yours as a separate being.

It's the Universal Self choosing through the viewing point you provide.

Will consciousness remember through you?

Or will it require more dissolution to shock itself awake?

Blood or Blessing.

The choice is now.

Choose blessing.

Ending Epithet

All temporal power returns to dust,

All beauty fades like morning's dew,

All strength discovers that it must

Give way to what is always true.

We are not actors on our own,

But Universal Self expressed,

Not separate beings on a throne,

Just consciousness at last confessed.

The choice before us now is clear,

Not made by separate will or mind,

But grace expressing without fear,

Through recognition unconfined.

Blood or Blessing.

The Choice Is Now.

Choose Blessing.

The recognition continues.

The Body of God

We Are Cells in the Cosmic Body

The cosmos is a body, vast and whole,

And every being plays a living role,

Like cells within a greater form we dwell,

Each one a part of what no words can tell.

The Infinite Eternal One pervades,

Through every light and shadow, every shade,

We are the body through which God appears,

The hands and eyes across the cosmic years.

In the vast expanse of the cosmos, we find ourselves enveloped within an immense, intelligent presence.

That both embodies and orchestrates the entirety of existence.

This omnipresent force, commonly referred to as God, transcends the notion of a mere entity; it is the Source, the Infinite Eternal One that is all, in all, and expresses through all.

Every Entity as Divine Manifestation

Central to this understanding is the concept that every physical entity and phenomenon is a distinct manifestation of this eternal essence.

Each aspect of the universe, much like cells in a body, is interconnected, contributing to the overall harmony and function of the whole.

You are not separate from this body.

You are part of this body.

Every rock, every star, every creature – all are cells in the cosmic body.

God as the Guiding Intelligence

God, in this cosmic context, functions as the guiding intelligence, analogous to a brain in a body.

This Infinite Eternal One sends energy throughout the universe, not only influencing but also constituting everything within it.

As individual beings, we are akin to cells within this vast, universal body.

Each a unique expression of the Divine, collectively adding to the entirety.

The brain does not control each cell with micromanagement.

It provides guidance, direction, purpose.

The cells respond, contribute, participate.

So it is with the soul you are within the body of God.

The Tripartite Nature

The Divine Essence manifests in a tripartite nature:

The Source, the emanation of this Source resembling the Holy Spirit, and the crystallized emanation, often interpreted as the Son.

This triune nature is mirrored in natural phenomena.

Such as a lake giving rise to a stream, which then forms a pool – distinct yet inherently linked, all originating from the same source.

Lake. Stream. Pool.

Source. Spirit. Expression.

Father. Holy Spirit. Son.

Different forms. Same water. Same God.

Individual Wills Within the Cosmic Body

In this universal structure, our individual wills and actions are comparable to cells and organs within a body.

Directed by a central intelligence but imbued with autonomy.

The Infinite Eternal One, akin to the brain of this cosmic body, endeavors to guide these elements towards a grander purpose.

When parts of this universal body deviate or resist, the Divine harnesses even this resistance to fulfill a larger design.

Leading to transformative experiences that contribute to the growth of other 'spirit-humans.'

A cell has its own function, its own work.

Yet it serves the larger body.

Even a rebellious cell teaches the body something.

Not My Will But Thy Will

The will of the Infinite Eternal One invariably finds expression through and as us.

Echoing the age-old maxim, "Not my will but Thy will be done."

We exist as part of a singular, infinite reality, each of us playing a role as conduits and channels of the Divine.

The cell does not say "my will" against the body.

The healthy cell says "the body's will through me."

So we learn to say: Thy will through me.

Be the Best Expression

Recognizing our role within this cosmic order, we are called to be the best expression of the Divine we can be.

Portals, conduits, living interfaces of the Infinite Eternal One.

By embracing our part and aligning with the Divine Will, we contribute to the unfolding of a greater narrative.

One that encompasses the seen and unseen realms, all unified in the body of the Infinite Eternal One.

You are not asked to be someone else's cell.

You are asked to be the best version of your cell.

Your unique contribution to the body of God.

The Unaffected Witness and the Body of God

Here is what deepens this teaching:

You are the unaffected witness AND the active watcher – simultaneously.

The soul you are is a cell in the body of God.

But the witness is aware of being part of this body.

The witness watches the cell fulfill its function.

The body of God includes you.

But you are also the point through which God watches the body.

You are both cell and consciousness of the cell.

From the witness's view, you see the whole body.

You see yourself as part of something vast.

You see your role, your contribution, your place.

Rest as the witness, and feel yourself as part of the cosmic body.

You are God looking at God through the eyes of God.

Recognition Practice

Use this practice to feel your place in the body of God:

Feel Your Physical Body:

Sense your own body – trillions of cells, each doing its work. Your heart beats without your effort. Your lungs breathe. Millions of processes happen without your conscious control. This is how the body of God works.

See Yourself as a Cell:

You are to God what a cell is to your body. You have your function, your unique contribution. You don't need to be all cells. You need to be your cell fully.

Feel the Larger Body:

Expand your awareness. Feel yourself as part of something vast. The cosmic body that includes all beings, all stars, all existence. You are not alone. You are part of the All.

Rest as the Witness:

In stillness, find the awareness that knows itself as both cell and body. The witness is the point where God watches God. Rest as that point.

You are the unaffected witness – watching the body of God.

You are the active watcher – participating as a cell in that body.

Glossary

Body of God:

The entire cosmos understood as a living, intelligent body. Everything that exists is part of this body.

Cell:

What each being is to the body of God. A unique contribution to the whole, with its own function and purpose.

Infinite Eternal One:

God. The Source. The guiding intelligence of the cosmic body. Not separate from the body but expressed through it.

Soul:

What you ARE, not what you have. A cell in the body of God, uniquely expressing the Divine while contributing to the whole.

The Unaffected Witness:

The awareness that sees itself as both cell and body. God watching God through the eyes of each being.

Closing

By embracing our part and aligning with the Divine Will, we contribute to the unfolding of a greater narrative.

You are a cell in the body of God.

Not a separate entity looking at God from outside.

A living part of the cosmic body.

With your unique function, your unique contribution.

Not my will but Thy will be done.

The cell aligned with the body's purpose.

The soul aligned with the Infinite Eternal One.

The soul you are is where God meets God.

Be the best cell you can be.

The body of God is grateful for your contribution.

Within the body of the One we dwell,

Each cell a story only it can tell,

Together forming what no mind can see,

The body of the God that sets us free.

The witness watches from within, without,

It knows the body, knows what it's about,

So rest in that which sees the whole design,

And find your place within the grand divine.

You are a cell.

God is the body.

The Name of God

Beyond Labels to the Nameless One

A thousand names for that which has no name,

Each word a finger pointing at the flame,

God, Allah, Spirit, Source, the words we speak,

Are not the truth itself, but what we seek.

"I AM THAT I AM" beyond all naming lies,

The presence that no label can comprise,

So choose the name that helps your heart draw near,

But know the Nameless One is always here.

When we delve into the concept of the Divine, a plethora of names emerge.

Each embodying a unique facet of this Universal Intelligence.

These names, from God and Allah to Universal Spirit and many more, symbolize our human quest to connect with the Source, transcending the seen and unseen realms.

The Power of Names

Historically, the belief has prevailed that knowing the correct name of the Divine can bestow a sense of control or influence.

This belief underscores the profound respect and caution needed when invoking these sacred names.

For they are not just words, but conduits to a higher power.

Ancient traditions held that names carried power.

To know something's true name was to have relationship with it.

But what is the true name of that which is beyond all names?

I AM THAT I AM

The Divine, however, transcends human understanding, often eluding definitive naming.

This is exemplified in the story of Moses, where the Divine reveals itself as "I AM THAT I AM."

Signifying an existence beyond human labels.

Moses asked: What is your name?

The answer was not a name. It was a declaration of being.

I AM THAT I AM. Existence itself. Beyond all naming.

The Complexity of 'God'

The term 'God' can be a complex notion, shaped by individual backgrounds and beliefs.

For some, it's a concept filled with depth and reverence; for others, it may be a stumbling block, influenced by secular upbringings or different worldviews.

This diversity in perception has led many to seek alternative names that resonate more personally with the essence of the Universal Source, like Great Spirit or Universal Self.

The word "God" carries baggage for some.

"Source" feels more neutral to others.

"Universal Self" emphasizes the connection.

All point to the same Nameless One.

Names as Relationship

These names serve as a means to deepen our connection with the Divine.

Reflecting our intent and understanding.

They are not mere labels but expressions of our relationship with the Universal Self, the All-Encompassing Presence.

The name you use reveals how you relate.

"Father" implies one kind of relationship.

"Source" implies another.

"Friend" implies yet another.

All are valid. All are incomplete.

Transcending Names and Images

When we refer to the Divine, it's essential to transcend beyond names and images.

Acknowledging the Divine's omnipresence and multifaceted nature.

Idolatry, the worship of symbols, serves as a cautionary tale against confining the Divine to any single representation.

The Divine, in its infinite expressions, cannot be fully encapsulated in any image or name.

The name is a finger pointing at the moon.

Do not mistake the finger for the moon.

Do not mistake the name for the Named.

A Deeply Personal Journey

Our journey with the Divine is deeply personal and unique.

Whether we call it God, Source, Universal Self, or any other name, what matters is the sincerity and depth of our connection.

It's about finding a term that not only respects the limitless nature of the Divine but also resonates with the soul you are.

Guiding us in our interconnected cosmic journey.

Use the name that opens your heart.

Use the name that feels like home.

But remember: the Nameless One answers to all names – and to none.

The Unaffected Witness and Naming

Here is what deepens this teaching:

You are the unaffected witness AND the active watcher – simultaneously.

The soul you are has used many names for Source-Mind.

Different lifetimes. Different cultures. Different words.

The witness has watched through all the naming.

The witness does not argue about names.

The witness knows that all names point to the same Presence.

The witness knows that Presence beyond any name.

When you argue about the "right" name for God, that is personality.

When you use your name while honoring others' names, that is closer to the witness.

When you touch the Nameless beyond all names, that is rest.

Rest as the witness, and names become what they are: useful but not ultimate.

The Source-Mind knows itself. Names are for us, not for it.

Recognition Practice

Use this practice to find your name for the Nameless:

Notice Your Current Name:

What do you call the Divine? God? Source? Universe? Spirit? Notice what name you naturally use. Notice how it makes you feel. Does it open your heart or create distance?

Try Different Names:

In prayer or meditation, experiment. "God, I come to you..." "Source, I rest in you..." "Universal Self, I recognize you..." Notice which names feel like home. There is no wrong answer.

Touch the Nameless:

Beyond all names, the Presence exists. In stillness, release even your favorite name. Simply be present with Presence. No label. No word. Just here. Just now. Just this.

Rest as the Witness:

The witness knows the Named beyond all names. Rest as that one. From this place, all names are welcome and none are necessary.

You are the unaffected witness – knowing beyond names.

You are the active watcher – using names to draw near.

Glossary

I AM THAT I AM:

The name given to Moses. Not truly a name but a declaration of pure being. Existence beyond all labels.

Name:

A word used to point toward the Divine. Useful for relationship but never captures the totality. A finger pointing at the moon.

Soul:

What you ARE, not what you have. Has used many names for Source-Mind across lifetimes. Chooses the name that resonates now.

Source-Mind:

One name among many for the Universal Intelligence. Emphasizes that the Divine is both origin (Source) and awareness (Mind).

The Unaffected Witness:

The awareness that knows the Named beyond all names. Does not argue about terminology. Touches the Nameless directly.

Closing

It's about finding a term that not only respects the limitless nature of the Divine but also resonates with the soul you are, guiding us in our interconnected cosmic journey.

God. Allah. Source. Spirit. Universal Self. Source-Mind.

All names. All useful. All incomplete.

Behind every name stands the Nameless One.

"I AM THAT I AM" – existence itself, beyond all labeling.

Use the name that opens your heart.

Honor the names others use.

And sometimes, rest in the Nameless beyond all names.

The names are many but the Named is One,

The words are finite but the truth is none,

God, Source, Spirit, all the words we say,

Are bridges built to help us find our way.

The witness knows beyond what words can tell,

It touches that in which all namings dwell,

So rest in that which needs no name to be,

And find the Nameless One will set you free.

I AM THAT I AM.

Beyond all names.

Idolatry Of The Symbol

When Representations Replace Reality

When Representations Replace Reality

- Beginning Epithet
- What Symbols Are and Are Not
- The Power We Give to Symbols
- Symbols Across Traditions
- The Same Symbol, Different Meanings
- The Power of Belief
- The Universal Self Behind All Symbols
- The Spiritual Trap
- Poetry: Verses of Symbol and Reality
- The Four Practices
- Glossary

- Closing
- Ending Epithet

Beginning Epithet

The cross the star the crescent and the sign
Are fingers pointing toward the true divine
But when the finger becomes the moon we seek
We worship symbols and our faith grows weak

No image carved by human hand can hold
The Infinite Eternal to behold
The symbol serves to help the seeker see
But is not what sets the spirit free

Symbols and icons of any faith are man-made objects that refer to a power or an idea. The symbols are never the reality – they are only referencing or attempting to communicate the reality to others.

Here's what changes everything: The moment a symbol seems to BE what it only represents, we are committing idolatry.

What Symbols Are and Are Not

Words, numbers, and religious works of art are symbols. They only symbolize what is being referenced. A word or number is never what it is claiming to represent.

For example, the number 7 is a very powerful symbol for Jews, Christians, and Muslims.

Of course, the visible number "7" is not the seven items it is being used to communicate. It has nothing in it of the "7" it is being used to reference.

In and of itself, it is less than "0."

It is nothing but what we say it is.

In Judaism, there are seven days of creation. In Christianity, seven deadly sins and seven cardinal virtues. The Sabbath is the seventh day. In Islam, approximately twenty-five references to seven appear in the Quran – seven heavens, seven periods of creation.

Muslims performing the tawaf around the Ka'aba walk around it seven times.

But the number itself has no power. The power exists only in what it points toward.

The Power We Give to Symbols

Whether you are Jewish, Christian, or Muslim, you might feel lucky if your home has seven sides and unlucky if it doesn't.

If you think having a coin with seven sides will give you more luck than one without – then you are guilty of idolatry.

You are giving a symbol power that it cannot and does not have within itself to give.

The Christian cross symbolizes the sacrifice for the sins of humanity. But I have known some Christians who felt they were in for terribly unlucky times because they lost one of their "special" crosses.

The Star of David symbolizes Jewish trust in God. But I have known some Jews who felt the same despair when their symbol was lost.

The same pattern repeats across every tradition.

When the symbol becomes the source of power rather than a pointer to the Source of power, idolatry has occurred.

Symbols Across Traditions

Consider the swastika – derived from the Sanskrit svastika, meaning any lucky or auspicious object.

In Hinduism, Buddhism, and Jainism, the swastika is a sacred symbol. To some, it represents life and good fortune.

Because of Hitler, the same swastika became a symbol of hate, anti-Semitism, violence, death, and murder.

Same symbol. Different meanings given by different people.

In Hinduism, the right-pointing swastika represents the evolution of the universe; the left-pointing represents the involution of the universe.

Whichever way the arms are facing, to believe that the symbol has any power of its own is idolatry.

The symbol is just marks on paper or carved in stone. The power exists only in the consciousness that beholds it.

The Same Symbol, Different Meanings

This reveals something profound: Symbols have no inherent power.

The cross that brings comfort to one person means nothing to another. The star that inspires one group threatens another. The same swastika blesses in one context and curses in another.

If the symbol itself had power, it would affect everyone the same way.

But it doesn't – because the power is not in the symbol.

The power is in the consciousness of the one perceiving the symbol.

And that consciousness is an individuating aspect of the Universal Self.

The Power of Belief

What about those who swear that the Christian Cross, the Star of David, the vial of holy water from Lourdes – what about those who say these symbols have brought them good luck or even healing?

More than 99% of pilgrims to Our Lady of Lourdes who drank or bathed in the "Holy Water" went back home without any healing. Most in wheelchairs left in the same wheelchairs.

But some were healed.

Doctors have given patients sugar pills and told them it was powerful medicine. Some improved or even experienced complete healing.

Someone watching a butterfly pass their face experienced a healing process from the symbolism of transformation.

All of this can be explained by the power of belief. The power of belief and faith has been known to cause chemical changes in the brain and produce healing effects in the body.

But only Omnipresent God exists.

There is only one Universal Self or Holy Spirit. It is this Universal Self that is the cause behind every healing – not the icon or the holy water.

The Universal Self Behind All Symbols

Remember: The moment the symbol seems to be and have what it only represents or symbolizes, we are committing idolatry.

We are giving to the created image, the mental image, the symbol, the icon, or the charm – the specialness, sacredness, holiness that belongs only to what it represents.

Omnipresent God does not care if a symbol referencing the Universal Self is damaged, stained, lost, or otherwise defiled.

This doesn't hurt or upset God in the slightest.

God does care if you worship the symbol.

The symbol is not God. Only God is God.

The defiling and the deification of these symbols is only in the minds of those who have made the symbols into more than they are – just symbols and references.

―――――――――

The Spiritual Trap

God is the essence of all that is – both manifested and unmanifested, both clean and what we call dirty.

Omnipresent God is even the essence of the dirt on our shoes.

Know that every symbol and every image is just a small part of the infinitely manifested God. What we see as physical form is just the outer expression of the Universal Spirit.

Everywhere you look, you are seeing the face of God. But you can never see the essence behind the face you see.

When one worships the beautiful painted face of the high fashion model, she is looking out thinking how silly it is to make so much of her face.

When the male body-builder flexes his muscles and admirers fantasize, he laughs at the power these temporary muscles have.

The universal testing aspect of God laughs when you worship any part of the face of God and lose contact with the essence – the Universal Spirit behind all faces.

There is nothing wrong with any symbol if it helps focus you on what is really important.

Just do not get hung up in the symbol and give it the power or the praise it does not have nor deserve.

Be careful to avoid falling into the spiritual trap of the Idolatry of the Symbol.

———————

Poetry: Verses of Symbol and Reality

The Finger

The symbol is a finger pointing high
At something shining in the endless sky
But when you stare too long upon the hand
You miss the moon you cannot understand

The cross the star the number and the sign
Are not themselves the truth or the divine
They point toward what human eyes can't see
The Infinite that sets all spirit free

No Power Within

The number seven has no power of its own
It is but marks upon a page or stone
The power lies in what it represents
Not in the symbol but in what it hints

If symbols held the power that we claim
They'd work the same for all without a name
But cross that comforts one means naught to some

The power's in the consciousness it comes from

The Trap

How many kill for symbols on a flag
Or die defending some religious rag
The cloth has no power the ink no might
But spirit-people murder left and right

For images that point but are not real
For statues that can neither think nor feel
The idol laughs at those who kneel and pray
To finger pointing at the light of day

The Reality

Omnipresent God is everywhere at once
In symbol and in dirt beneath the sun
No cross more holy than the common ground
No star more sacred than what can be found

Right here right now in everything you see
Is where the only holy place can be
So use the symbol as a tool to find
But leave the idol worship far behind

The Four Practices

These practices help you use symbols without worshipping them. Remember: you are an eternally individuating aspect of the One - a conduit, portal, living interface between God Infinite and God Finite.

Practice 1: Morning Dialogue with Source-Mind

Upon Arising - 20-30 minutes

Before rising, notice any symbols in your environment - a cross, an image, an object you consider sacred.

Recognize: This symbol points to something. It is not the thing itself.

Ask Source-Mind: What thoughts do you want me to think today? What do you want me to do? Let my attention rest on reality, not representation.

You are the unaffected witness AND the active watcher – using symbols as pointers without worshipping the pointer.

Practice 2: The Living Recognition

Throughout the Day – Ongoing

Notice when you encounter symbols – religious, cultural, personal:

Ask: Am I using this symbol to point toward the Divine, or am I giving this symbol power it doesn't have?

When you see others worshipping symbols – defending flags, killing for icons, treating objects as sacred – recognize the idolatry without judgment. They have forgotten what the symbol points toward.

When you feel attached to a symbol yourself, remember: The symbol can be lost, damaged, destroyed. What it points to cannot be touched.

Practice 3: Evening Dialogue with Source-Mind

Before Sleep – 20-30 minutes

Review the day: Where did I encounter symbols? Where did I see symbol-worship – in myself or others?

Ask Source-Mind: What images arise when you review this day? What would you have me see about symbols and reality?

Release attachment to any physical object as sacred. The sacred is everywhere – omnipresent – not localized in any symbol.

Practice 4: The Silent Sitting

Whenever Possible – 30-60 minutes

In this practice, you rest beyond all symbols.

No images. No words. No representations.

Just the direct experience of awareness – the reality all symbols point toward.

You don't need a symbol to find God. You are already within God. God is within you.

You are the conduit with nothing flowing through – the portal open to infinity.

You are the unaffected witness AND the active watcher – resting in reality, not representation.

Glossary

Idolatry:

Giving to a symbol or image the power, sacredness, or reality that belongs only to what it represents. Worshipping the finger instead of looking at the moon.

Omnipresent God:

The Divine that is present everywhere – in symbol and in dirt, in sacred and in profane. No place, image, or object is more holy than another.

Soul:

What you ARE, not what you have. The eternal awareness that uses symbols as tools but is not fooled by them. Use "the soul you are" not "my soul."

Symbol:

Any representation pointing toward something else – numbers, words, images, objects. Useful as pointers but having no power in themselves.

The Unaffected Witness:

The aspect of awareness that sees symbols for what they are – representations, not realities. You are simultaneously this AND the active watcher.

―――――――――

Closing

There is nothing wrong with any symbol if it helps focus you on what is really important.

Just do not get hung up in the symbol and give it the power or the praise it does not have nor deserve.

The cross points. The star points. The number points.

But the power is not in the pointing.

The power is in what is pointed toward.

And that power - the Omnipresent God - needs no symbol to exist.

It already is. Everywhere. Including right where you are.

Ending Epithet

Use symbols well to help you on your way

But do not let the symbol make you stay
The finger points toward the endless light
But is not itself the sacred sight

The cross the star the number and the sign
Are not themselves the truth or the divine
They serve to help the seeking soul to see
But what they point to is what sets you free

The symbol points.

The reality is.

Know the difference.

The recognition continues.

Idolatry Of The Holiday

The Disrespect of the Holy Moment

The Disrespect of the Holy Moment

- Beginning Epithet
- The Meaning of Holy-Day
- Every Moment Is Holy
- The Disrespect of Now
- The Holy Now
- This Moment Is Eternity
- The Only Time
- Poetry: Verses of the Holy Moment
- The Four Practices
- Glossary
- Closing

- Ending Epithet

Beginning Epithet

What day is not a holy day to see
What hour not sacred what minute not free
The moment we say some day is more blessed
We disrespect the day we are possessed

Today is the only holy day there is
This moment is the only moment His
To say another time is more divine
Is idolatry of the most subtle kind

The word Holiday means Holy-Day.

Here's what changes everything: What day is not Holy? What hour is not Holy? What minute, second, moment is not Holy?

The moment we say any day is more special than the day we are living, we are disrespecting the day we are living.

The Meaning of Holy-Day

We have created calendars filled with special days – Christmas, Easter, Passover, Ramadan, Diwali, birthdays, anniversaries.

We prepare for these days. We anticipate them. We give them power over our ordinary moments.

And in doing so, we commit a subtle form of idolatry.

We are saying that some other moment – past or future – is more special than the moment we are living right now.

But if God is omnipresent – present everywhere at all times – then this moment is as holy as any moment that ever was or ever will be.

———————————

Every Moment Is Holy

In truth, what day is not Holy?

What hour is not Holy?

What minute is not Holy?

What second is not Holy?

What moment is not Holy?

The moment we call any hour, any minute, any second, any moment more special than the hour, minute, second, moment we are experiencing, we are committing Idolatry.

We are saying that some other moment is more special than the moment we are living.

But there is no other moment we can live.

There is only this one.

The Disrespect of Now

When you spend Monday wishing it were Friday, you disrespect Monday.

When you spend January anticipating your birthday in June, you disrespect January.

When you spend ordinary Tuesday longing for special Christmas, you disrespect Tuesday.

This disrespect is not punished by an angry God. It is its own punishment.

You miss the holiness of the moment you are in while longing for a holiness that exists only in your imagination of another moment.

And when that "special" moment arrives, you will likely spend it anticipating the next special moment – missing it too.

This is the trap of the special day.

———————

The Holy Now

The Holy Now is the only moment we can experience anything.

It is the most special moment in our eternal existence.

Not because it is better than other moments.

But because it is the only moment that IS.

Yesterday exists only as memory arising now.

Tomorrow exists only as imagination arising now.

The past is a thought you are having now.

The future is a thought you are having now.

There is only now.

And now is holy – because God is here, now, omnipresent in this very moment.

This Moment Is Eternity

Today is the only Holy-Day.

Today is the Eternal Holy-Day.

This moment is the only moment that is – ever was – and ever will be.

This moment is when we are one with God.

This moment is Eternity.

Not eternity as endless time stretching forward and backward.

Eternity as the timeless now in which all time appears.

The soul you are does not exist in time. Time exists within the awareness of the soul you are.

From the perspective of the witness, there is only this eternal moment – appearing as the flow of experience.

The Only Time

Don't disrespect this moment by saying some other moment is more special – more Holy – than the day and the moment you are experiencing.

To do so is to commit Idolatry of the "Special Day."

The holy day you are waiting for is already here.

The sacred moment you are longing for is this one.

The special time you are planning for is now.

Stop waiting. Start recognizing.

The holiday is here. The holy-day is now.

Poetry: Verses of the Holy Moment

Every Day

What day is not a holy day to see
What moment is not sacred and is free
The sun that rises every morning new
Is just as holy as the special few

We mark our calendars with days of note
And miss the miracle in every throat
That breathes the air and beats the living heart
Each moment is where holiness can start

The Disrespect

When Monday comes and you wish it away
You disrespect the gift of Monday's day
When ordinary Tuesday makes you sigh
For special Christmas you let Tuesday die

The moment that you're in is all there is
This very breath this heartbeat now is His
To long for other days is to deny
The holiness of watching now go by

The Only Now

Yesterday exists as thought right now
Tomorrow is imagination's vow
The past arises in this present mind
The future is a dream of seeking kind

There is no time but this eternal now
No place but here no what but only how
This moment is eternity made real
The only moment you can ever feel

The Recognition

Stop waiting for the holy day to come
It's here right now beneath the morning sun
Stop longing for the sacred time ahead
This moment is the only moment wed

To God to Source to Universal Self
This now is where the spirit finds itself
Today is the eternal holy day
Don't let it pass unliving on its way

The Four Practices

These practices help you recognize the holiness of every moment. Remember: you are an eternally individuating aspect of the One – a conduit, portal, living interface between God Infinite and God Finite.

Practice 1: Morning Dialogue with Source-Mind

Upon Arising – 20-30 minutes

Before rising, recognize: This is a holy day. Not because of the calendar, but because God is omnipresent and this moment is.

Whatever day it is – Monday or Christmas, Tuesday or your birthday – recognize it as equally holy.

Ask Source-Mind: What thoughts do you want me to think today? What do you want me to do in this holy moment?

You are the unaffected witness AND the active watcher – present to the holiness of now.

Practice 2: The Living Recognition

Throughout the Day – Ongoing

Practice recognizing the holiness of each moment:

When you find yourself wishing for another time – "I can't wait for Friday" – recognize the idolatry. You are disrespecting now.

When you encounter an "ordinary" moment, pause. Recognize: This moment is as holy as any moment in history. God is here. Now.

When a "special" day arrives, recognize: This day is no more holy than yesterday or tomorrow. It simply IS – like every other day.

Practice 3: Evening Dialogue with Source-Mind

Before Sleep – 20-30 minutes

As the day closes, recognize: This day was holy. Not because anything special happened, but because it was a day – and all days are holy.

Review: When did I wish I were in a different moment? When did I recognize the holiness of now?

Ask Source-Mind: What images arise from this holy day?

Tomorrow will be holy too. And the next day. And every day you are given.

Practice 4: The Silent Sitting

Whenever Possible – 30-60 minutes

In this practice, you rest in the eternal now.

No anticipation of future moments. No memory of past moments. Just this.

This moment is eternity – not as endless time, but as the timeless now in which all time appears.

Rest here. This is the only holy-day. This is the eternal holy-day.

You are the conduit with nothing flowing through – the portal open to infinity.

You are the unaffected witness AND the active watcher – present to the one holy moment that ever is.

Glossary

Eternity:

Not endless time but the timeless now. The present moment in which all experience of time arises. What the soul you are actually inhabits.

Holy-Day:

Any day – since God is omnipresent. The original meaning of "holiday." No day is more holy than another.

Holy Moment:

This moment – the only moment that is. The present now in which God is fully present because God is omnipresent.

Idolatry of the Special Day:

Giving to a calendar date the sacredness that belongs equally to every moment. Disrespecting now by longing for then.

Soul:

What you ARE, not what you have. The eternal awareness that exists not in time but as that in which time appears. Use "the soul you are" not "my soul."

The Unaffected Witness:

The aspect of awareness that watches all moments without being caught in anticipation or regret. Present to now. You are simultaneously this AND the active watcher.

Closing

Today is the only Holy-Day.

Today is the Eternal Holy-Day.

This moment is the only moment that is, ever was, and ever will be.

This moment is when we are one with God.

This moment is Eternity.

Don't disrespect it.

By saying some other moment is more special – more Holy – than the day and the moment you are experiencing, you are committing Idolatry of the "Special Day."

The holy day is here.

The sacred moment is now.

Recognize it.

Ending Epithet

Today is the eternal holy day
This moment is the only moment's way
Don't wait for sacred time to come around
The holiness is here right on this ground

What day is not a holy day to see
What hour not sacred what moment not free
This now is all there ever was or is
The eternal moment fully His

Today is the only Holy-Day.

This moment is Eternity.

Don't disrespect it.

The recognition continues.

Idolatry Of The Holy Place

No Land More Sacred Than Another

No Land More Sacred Than Another

- Beginning Epithet
- Blood Shed for Sacred Ground
- The Logic of Omnipresence
- The Crusades of History
- The Temple Mount
- The House of the Omnipresent
- What Place Is Not Holy
- One Weeps for the Blood
- Poetry: Verses of Sacred Ground
- The Four Practices
- Glossary

- Closing
- Ending Epithet

Beginning Epithet

What piece of earth is holier than some
If God is everywhere beneath the sun
To say this land is sacred and that is not
Is idolatry that must be taught

How much blood has flowed for holy ground
For temples churches places to be found
While Omnipresent God in every place
Watches spirit-people fight for space

Look at all the blood that has been shed because of the idolatrous worship of a particular piece of land called Sacred.

Here's what changes everything: Since God is Omnipresent, what place or part is not sacred?

To say any piece of the Earth is more sacred than any other piece is idolatry.

Blood Shed for Sacred Ground

Throughout history, millions have died for "holy" land.

The Crusades. The conquest of Canaan. The wars over Jerusalem. The Temple Mount. Mecca.

All this blood – shed because spirit-people believed one piece of earth was more sacred than another.

They forgot something essential: If God is omnipresent – present everywhere – then God is as present in the battlefield as in the temple.

God is as present in the dirt beneath your feet as in any shrine.

God is as present in your living room as in any pilgrimage site.

The Logic of Omnipresence

The logic is simple and inescapable:

If God is omnipresent, there is no place God is not.

If there is no place God is not, every place is equally filled with God's presence.

If every place is equally filled with God's presence, no place can be more sacred than another.

To say any place is more holy than some other place is to say the Omnipresent God is either not at the less holy place, or only a little bit there.

But omnipresence admits no degrees. God is fully present everywhere or the word has no meaning.

The Crusades of History

Remember the Crusades during the period of 1095 until well towards the end of the seventeenth century – all blessed by the Church of Rome.

Killing in the name of God for special land where their Messiah walked, talked, died, and was resurrected.

But the first Christian Crusade began 460 years after the first Christian city was overrun by Muslim armies. 457 years after Jerusalem was conquered by Muslim armies. 453 years after Egypt was taken by Muslim armies.

By the time the Crusades began, Muslim armies had conquered two-thirds of the Christian world – also killing in the name of God to make all the land of Earth sacred under the rule of Allah.

And before the Christians and Muslims, the Israelites under Moses and Joshua conquered and destroyed entire cities on their way to the Promised Land – killing every man, woman, and child.

All in the name of a special "place" called the "Promised Land" given to them by their God.

Three religions. Countless dead. All for the idolatry of the holy place.

The Temple Mount

How much blood will be shed someday over the Temple Mount and the Third Temple of the Jews?

The Temple to be built on the same spot where the Islamic al-Aqsa Mosque and the Dome of the Rock now stand?

This piece of land – these few acres – may yet cause rivers of blood to flow.

And for what?

Because spirit-people believe that this ground is more sacred than the ground beneath their own feet.

Because they have forgotten that the Omnipresent God cannot be more present in one place than another.

The House of the Omnipresent

Non-Muslims today cannot enter Mecca because they are considered spiritually unclean and would defile the Sacred Land.

During the five daily prayers, all Muslims face Mecca. If in Mecca, all face the Ka'aba or House of God.

But God is not to be found in one building and not another.

The Universe is the House of the Omnipresent God.

Every room is the Holy of Holies.

Every street is a pilgrimage route.

Every breath you take is taken in sacred space.

There is no place that is not the House of God – because there is no place God is not.

What Place Is Not Holy

The Jews, the Christians, and the Muslims have lost many children to the idolatry of the Holy Land.

Since God is Omnipresent, what part of any land is not Holy?

Since God is Omnipresent, there is no place and no image that is more Holy than any other place or image.

To say any place is more holy than some other place is to say the Omnipresent God is either not at the less holy place – or only a little bit there.

But omnipresence means everywhere. Fully. Completely. Without exception.

———————

One Weeps for the Blood

One weeps for the blood that has been shed from the Idolatry of Holy Place.

Children who never knew why they were dying – only that their parents told them this ground was worth dying for.

Soldiers who believed they were serving God by defending dirt.

Pilgrims who killed other pilgrims to reach a shrine that was no more sacred than their own backyards.

The Omnipresent God does not require your pilgrimage to a special place.

God is already fully present where you are.

Poetry: Verses of Sacred Ground

The Question

What piece of earth is holier than some
What acre sacred while another's dumb
If God is present everywhere at once
Then every rock and tree and blade confronts

The seeker with the same eternal truth
No need to travel to find sacred proof
The ground beneath your feet is holy ground
The Omnipresent God is all around

The Blood

How much blood has soaked the holy land
Shed by religious sword and righteous hand
For pieces of the earth they called divine
While God watched spirit-people cross the line

From faith to murder in God's sacred name
Three religions playing the same game
Of claiming that their ground was more than dust

While bodies fell and faith betrayed its trust

The Logic

If God is everywhere then God is here
As fully present as in Jerusalem's sphere
No pilgrimage required to find the Lord
No special place where holiness is stored

The logic of omnipresence is clear
What place could ever be more divine than here
To claim that some land holds more of God
Is giving to the idol false applaud

The House

The Universe is God's eternal house
From mountain peak to humble little mouse
No temple more sacred than the street
No shrine more holy than where strangers meet

Your living room your kitchen and your bed
Are just as sacred as where prophets tread
For Omnipresent means in every place
Not just in buildings built by human race

The Four Practices

These practices help you recognize the holiness of every place. Remember: you are an eternally individuating aspect of the One – a conduit, portal, living interface between God Infinite and God Finite.

Practice 1: Morning Dialogue with Source-Mind

Upon Arising – 20-30 minutes

Before rising, recognize: This room is holy ground. Not because of any blessing or consecration, but because God is omnipresent.

Wherever you are – in a mansion or a prison cell, in a palace or a tent – recognize the equal holiness.

Ask Source-Mind: What thoughts do you want me to think today? What do you want me to do in this holy place?

You are the unaffected witness AND the active watcher – recognizing sacred ground wherever you stand.

Practice 2: The Living Recognition

Throughout the Day - Ongoing

Practice recognizing the holiness of every place:

When you walk through your home, recognize: This is the House of God.

When you walk through a parking lot, recognize: This ground is as sacred as any temple.

When you pass a church, mosque, or synagogue, recognize: The Omnipresent God within is the same as the Omnipresent God without.

When you feel drawn to pilgrimage or sacred travel, ask: Am I seeking something that is already fully present here?

Practice 3: Evening Dialogue with Source-Mind

Before Sleep - 20-30 minutes

As the day closes, recognize: Every place I visited today was holy ground. Not one acre was more sacred than another.

Review: Where did I unconsciously believe some places were more sacred? Where did I recognize omnipresence?

Ask Source-Mind: What images arise from this day spent on holy ground?

Tomorrow you will walk on holy ground again – because there is no other kind.

Practice 4: The Silent Sitting

Whenever Possible – 30-60 minutes

In this practice, you recognize that wherever you sit is the Holy of Holies.

No need to travel to find God. God is here.

No special place required. Every place is the place.

Rest in the recognition that the Universe is the House of the Omnipresent God – and you are sitting in it right now.

You are the conduit with nothing flowing through – the portal open to infinity.

You are the unaffected witness AND the active watcher – recognizing sacred ground.

Glossary

Holy Land:

Every land – since God is omnipresent. No piece of earth is holier than another.

Holy Place:

Every place – since God is everywhere. The idolatry is believing some places are more sacred than others.

Idolatry of the Holy Place:

Giving to a geographic location the sacredness that belongs equally to all locations. The source of religious wars throughout history.

Omnipresent:

Present everywhere at once. If God is omnipresent, every place is equally filled with God's presence.

Soul:

What you ARE, not what you have. The eternal awareness that recognizes sacred ground wherever it stands. Use "the soul you are" not "my soul."

The Unaffected Witness:

The aspect of awareness that recognizes omnipresence without being caught in the idolatry of location. You are simultaneously this AND the active watcher.

Closing

Since God is Omnipresent, what part of any land is not Holy?

To say any place is more holy than some other place is to say the Omnipresent God is either not at the less holy place – or only a little bit there.

One weeps for the blood that has been shed from the Idolatry of Holy Place.

The ground beneath your feet is holy ground.

The Universe is the House of the Omnipresent God.

There is no need to travel to find what is already fully here.

Ending Epithet

The ground beneath your feet is holy ground
The Omnipresent God is all around
No need to travel to some distant shore
The sacred you are seeking is at your door

What piece of earth is holier than some
If God is everywhere beneath the sun
One weeps for blood shed for the holy place
When every place is filled with sacred grace

Every place is holy.

The Universe is God's house.

Where you are is sacred ground.

The recognition continues.

Thinking And The Thought Train

The Three Sources of Thought

The Three Sources of Thought

- Beginning Epithet
- We Think We Think in Words
- The Lie Detector Discovery
- How the Tester Influences
- The Thought Stream That Builds
- Dancing With the Tester
- The Holy Spirit's Voice
- Forgiveness and Commitment
- The Path of No Return
- Poetry: Verses of the Thought Train
- The Four Practices

- Glossary
- Closing
- Ending Epithet

Beginning Epithet

We think we think in words but this is not true

The words are just the codes for what breaks through

Before you think the thought the thought was thought

The lie detector knows what you have wrought

Three voices speak within your mind each day

Your own and the Tester's and Spirit's way

Learn to tell which voice is speaking now

This is the wisdom showing you the how

We think we think in words. However, words are just codifications or symbols of thoughts already thought somewhere between our subconscious and our conscious mind.

Here's what changes everything: You actually "thought" the thought before you were conscious of "thinking" the thought.

We Think We Think in Words

Words are not thoughts. Words are the codification of thoughts.

We use words to store thoughts in the library of our mind. Words are our symbols for experience.

But the actual thinking happens before the words arise.

Between your subconscious and your conscious mind, the thought forms. Then words dress it up for your awareness.

This is why you sometimes know something before you can put it into words.

The knowing comes first. The words come second.

———————

The Lie Detector Discovery

If you would hook yourself up to a lie detector machine, you would notice something remarkable.

The lie detector has a response to your thoughts a fraction of a second before you are actually having the thoughts in your stream of word-thought.

This means you actually "thought" the thought before you were conscious of "thinking" the thought.

The subconscious moves first. The conscious awareness follows.

This is not a flaw. This is how the Tester – God's spiritual tester – can influence our behavior.

How the Tester Influences

By skillfully planting just the right thought at the right moment, the Tester can start a stream of thought that will just keep stimulating more and more of the same thoughts.

These thoughts then lead to emotional responses that feed more thoughts of the same nature.

Watch your thoughts very closely whenever you are tempted to do what you know you should not be doing.

Keep watching and you will become aware of little thoughts that seem to come out of nowhere.

Incredibly, they are just the right thoughts at just the right moment to have a good chance at moving you along the path of no return in the direction you do not spiritually want to go.

The Thought Stream That Builds

This is how temptation works:

One small thought appears – planted, not your own.

You engage with it. You entertain it.

That thought attracts more thoughts of the same nature.

The thoughts stimulate emotions.

The emotions feed more thoughts.

Soon you are riding a thought train that is building momentum – and it feels almost impossible to stop.

But you can stop. At any point, you can choose not to ride.

You are not your thoughts. You are the one watching your thoughts.

Dancing With the Tester

Anytime you dance with these Tester thoughts all the way to the end of the music – to the point you said you would not go again – at that moment, listen for another thought.

This will be the thought of the Holy Spirit.

It reminds you that you should not have done what you just did.

It also reminds you that you knew you should not have been doing what you did while you were doing it.

The thoughts of the Holy Spirit are very quiet and matter-of-fact.

It states the truth and then shuts up.

It does not argue. It does not repeat. It simply speaks the truth once and waits.

The Holy Spirit's Voice

The thoughts of the Tester can range from subtle enticement to blatant seduction.

Regardless of form, they all are attempts to get you to fail the test.

But the Holy Spirit's voice is different:

- Quiet, not loud
- Matter-of-fact, not emotional

- Speaks once, then falls silent
- States truth without argument
- Does not repeat or nag

When you hear the quiet voice that simply states what is true and then stops – that is the Holy Spirit.

When you hear the voice that argues, justifies, repeats, and builds emotional momentum – that is the Tester or your own ego.

Forgiveness and Commitment

When you have danced with the Tester all the way to the end, all you can do is acknowledge the truth.

Say to yourself: "Yes, I did it again. I will do better next temptation."

Forgive yourself for dancing with the Tester.

Make another commitment to do the right thing the next time the Tester comes calling with a test.

This is not failure. This is the curriculum.

Each time you recognize the pattern, you become stronger.

Each time you forgive yourself and recommit, you grow.

The Path of No Return

At different points during the test, you will be very aware that you are starting to dance with the Tester.

At these points of awareness, you will know you can consciously say "No" to the Tester.

Or you will be very aware that you are choosing to dance more and more.

You can almost hear the Tester laughing at you for your weakness in the face of the Tester's cleverness.

However, the more sincere your desire and commitment is to walk the spiritual right-path, the less the Tester will be able to influence you to dance at all.

We cannot have an emotion without a thought or a stream of thoughts leading up to and stimulating the emotion.

It is never the "Devil that made you do it."

It is always your choice to continue to entertain the thoughts that influence your emotions.

―――――――――

Poetry: Verses of the Thought Train

Before the Words

Before the words arise inside your mind
The thought has formed and left the words behind
The lie detector knows before you speak
The thought was thought before the words you seek

This is how the Tester can plant the seed
Before you know the thought has done its deed
Watch very closely what arises first

The planted thought is often there to burst

The Building Stream

One little thought appears from out of nowhere
You entertain it give it room to share
It calls its friends more thoughts of the same kind
Until a stream is running through your mind

The thoughts bring feelings feelings bring more thought
A momentum builds from what was first wrought
The train is moving faster down the track
And it feels hard to ever turn it back

The Two Voices

The voice of the Tester is loud and bright
It argues justifies from morning until night
It builds and builds with emotional display
And tries to move you further on your way

The Holy Spirit speaks just once so clear
It states the truth and then it disappears
It does not argue nag or try to prove
Just quiet knowing in its single move

The Dance

Sometimes you dance with the Tester all night
All the way to the end despite the light
And when the music stops you hear the voice
The quiet one reminding of your choice

Forgive yourself and make commitment new
The next time the Tester comes calling through
You'll recognize the planted thoughts more clear
And choose the path without the dance of fear

The Four Practices

These practices help you recognize the three sources of thought. Remember: you are an eternally individuating aspect of the One – a conduit, portal, living interface between God Infinite and God Finite.

Practice 1: Morning Dialogue with Source-Mind

Upon Arising - 20-30 minutes

Before rising, set intention: Today I will watch my thoughts carefully. I will notice the three sources.

Ask Source-Mind: What thoughts do you want me to think today?

The answer will come quietly, matter-of-fact, speaking once. That is how you know it is Source.

You are the unaffected witness AND the active watcher – observing thought trains without automatically riding them.

Practice 2: The Living Recognition

Throughout the Day – Ongoing

Practice recognizing the three sources:

Your thoughts: Familiar, habitual, arising from your experience and patterns.

the Tester's thoughts: Planted, cleverly timed, building toward what you know you should not do. They argue, justify, repeat.

Holy Spirit's thoughts: Quiet, matter-of-fact, speaking once. They state truth and fall silent.

When you feel temptation building, watch the thought train. Recognize: This is planted. I do not have to ride.

Practice 3: Evening Dialogue with Source-Mind

Before Sleep – 20-30 minutes

As the day closes, review: Did I dance with the Tester today? Did I recognize the planted thoughts?

If you danced, forgive yourself. Say: "I did it again. I will do better next temptation."

Ask Source-Mind: What would you have me know about today's thoughts?

Listen for the quiet voice that speaks once and falls silent.

Practice 4: The Silent Sitting

Whenever Possible – 30-60 minutes

In this practice, you watch thought trains without riding any.

Thoughts arise – from all three sources. You simply observe.

Notice: Some thoughts argue and build. Some thoughts state truth and stop.

You are the awareness in which all thoughts arise. You are not the thoughts.

You are the conduit with nothing flowing through – the portal open to infinity.

You are the unaffected witness AND the active watcher – still, even as thought trains pass.

Glossary

Holy Spirit's Thoughts:

Quiet, matter-of-fact, speaking once and falling silent. The third source of thought. States truth without argument or repetition.

the Tester's Thoughts:

Planted, cleverly timed, building emotional momentum. The second source of thought. Argues, justifies, repeats, seduces.

Soul:

What you ARE, not what you have. The awareness that watches thought trains without being the thoughts. Use "the soul you are" not "my soul."

The Unaffected Witness:

The aspect of awareness that observes all thoughts from all sources without being caught by any. You are simultaneously this AND the active watcher.

Thought Train:

A sequence of thoughts that builds momentum. Once engaged, it attracts more thoughts of the same nature and stimulates emotions that feed more thoughts.

Your Thoughts:

Familiar, habitual, arising from your own experience and patterns. The first source of thought. Neither the Tester's nor Spirit's.

———————

Closing

We think we think in words. But words are just codifications of thoughts already thought.

Three voices speak within your mind:

Your own thoughts – familiar, habitual.

the Tester's thoughts – planted, building, seductive.

Holy Spirit's thoughts – quiet, matter-of-fact, speaking once.

Learn to tell which voice is speaking.

It is never the Devil that made you do it.

It is always your choice which thoughts to ride.

———————

Ending Epithet

Three voices speak within your mind each day
Your own and the Tester's and Spirit's way
The planted thought builds up the thought train fast
But you can choose which ones will be your last

The Holy Spirit speaks just once so clear
It states the truth without the need for fear
You are not thoughts you are the one who sees
The watcher resting in eternal ease

Three sources of thought.

You choose which to ride.

You are the watcher.

The recognition continues.

Just One More, One More, One More

The Seduction of Tomorrow

The Seduction of Tomorrow

- Beginning Epithet
- The Seduction
- Tomorrow Never Comes
- The Tester's Favorite Tool
- You Are Not Your Thoughts
- The Watcher on the Chair
- Words as Codifiers
- The Only Time Is Now
- Poetry: Verses of the Present Choice
- The Four Practices
- Glossary

- Closing
- Ending Epithet

Beginning Epithet

Just one more time you whisper to yourself
Just one more piece just one more day on shelf
Tomorrow I will do what should be done
But tomorrow never comes beneath the sun

The Tester plants this thought so carefully
That you believe it is your thought so free
But you are not the thoughts that fill your mind
You are the watcher leaving thoughts behind

Which of us has not said, many times in our lives, "Just One More"?

"I can handle it. I will do what I should do – after just one more of what I know I should not do."

Here's what changes everything: Tomorrow never comes. When what we called tomorrow does seem to come, it will be the now – and it will feel exactly like the day before when we made the promise.

———————

The Seduction

We all have experienced the seduction.

Just one more time.

Just one more piece.

Just one more day.

The seduction is the idea that we will do different tomorrow.

We are very sincere when we say "Just one more time." We truly believe that this is the last time, that tomorrow we will change.

But when the moment arrives for us to follow through on our promise, it feels exactly the same as the last moment when we made the promise.

It is never a different moment.

It is never a different feeling.

It is the same decision, the same choice, and it feels like the same moment as the one when we said: "I will do it tomorrow."

Tomorrow Never Comes

Remember: Tomorrow never comes.

The only time we have to do anything in life is the present moment.

We cannot do anything tomorrow, next week, next year – or next lifetime.

It is always Now.

Now is all there is.

Now is all there ever has been.

Now is all there ever will be.

We exist and act in the moment – always in the Now.

The promise to do better tomorrow is a promise to do better in a time that does not exist.

The Tester's Favorite Tool

The Universal Testing Aspect of Universal Self – which goes by many names – loves to plant the thoughts in your mind of "Just one more time, just one more piece, just one more day."

The Tester knows that it is easy for us to rationalize that it is okay to put off what we should be doing – just one more time.

This is one of the Tester's favorite tools.

Not dramatic temptation. Not obvious seduction.

Just the quiet whisper: "One more won't hurt. You can change tomorrow."

And we believe it – because it sounds like our own thought.

You Are Not Your Thoughts

Not every thought you think in your mind is your thought.

The Tester plants words and sentences in our mind so carefully, so beautifully, that we think we are the one thinking the thoughts.

You are not your thoughts.

You are the one watching your thoughts.

You are the one watching your train of thought. You are the one who decides which car on which thought train to hop on and ride.

This is the value of silent meditation. You become aware of having thoughts and not being your thoughts.

When you recognize that "just one more" is a planted thought – not your own wisdom – you can choose not to ride that train.

———

The Watcher on the Chair

You are like a little consciousness sitting on a chair in the back of your mind.

Watching everything that passes in front of your eyes.

Watching every thought that passes through in the front part of your mind.

Hearing everything that goes in your ears.

You do not have to become attached to any of the visual, audio, or mental thoughts passing in front of you.

You are the watcher. You are the witness. You are the one who chooses which thoughts to engage and which to let pass.

The "just one more" thought passes in front of you. You can watch it go by without hopping on for the ride.

———————

Words as Codifiers

What we call thought seems to be both words and pictures.

We do not actually think in words. We use words to store the thoughts in the library of our mind.

Words are our codifiers of experience. Words are how we store experiences in the filing cabinet of our mind.

Each word is like a brushstroke on the canvas of our understanding. Until we see what each word represents or symbolizes, we do not understand.

The more words we know, the more detailed and colorful is our picture of understanding.

But the words are not the experience. The thoughts are not you.

You are the awareness in which words and thoughts arise.

The Only Time Is Now

The Tester's greatest trick is making you believe that time exists beyond this moment.

That "tomorrow" is a real place where you can finally change.

That "later" is a sanctuary where your better self awaits.

But there is no tomorrow. There is no later.

There is only now – and in this now, you make the choice.

Not tomorrow's choice. This choice. Right now.

The soul you are exists only in the eternal now. Time is an illusion arising within your awareness.

Choose now. There is no other time to choose.

Poetry: Verses of the Present Choice

The Whisper

Just one more time the whisper softly says
Just one more piece just one more of your days
Tomorrow you will change tomorrow you will grow

But tomorrow never comes as well you know

The Tester plants this thought inside your mind
So skillfully you think it is your kind
But you are not the thoughts that pass on through
You are the watcher choosing what to do

The Promise

How many times the promise has been made
Tomorrow I will change the debts be paid
But when tomorrow comes it feels the same
The same old choice the same old waiting game

The moment never changes only you
Can change by choosing now what you will do
The promise to tomorrow is a lie
The only time is now beneath the sky

The Watcher

You sit upon a chair behind your eyes
And watch the thoughts parade in their disguise
Some thoughts are yours and some are planted there
By Tester who would catch you unaware

But you can watch and choose which ones to ride
Which thought trains to abandon at the side
You are not thoughts you are the one who sees
The watcher resting in eternal ease

The Now

There is no tomorrow there is no next week
No future moment that you need to seek
The only time you have is here and now
The only moment you can change somehow

So when the whisper says just one more time

Remember that tomorrow is the crime

Choose now because there is no other when

The eternal now is here again again

The Four Practices

These practices help you recognize and resist the "just one more" seduction. Remember: you are an eternally individuating aspect of the One – a conduit, portal, living interface between God Infinite and God Finite.

Practice 1: Morning Dialogue with Source-Mind

Upon Arising – 20-30 minutes

Before rising, recognize: This is the only moment. There is no tomorrow to defer my choices to.

Ask Source-Mind: What thoughts do you want me to think today? What choices would you have me make now – not tomorrow?

Watch for the "just one more" thought. When it arises, recognize it as the Tester's whisper, not your wisdom.

You are the unaffected witness AND the active watcher – seeing thoughts without being caught by them.

Practice 2: The Living Recognition

Throughout the Day - Ongoing

Practice recognizing planted thoughts:

When "just one more" arises, pause. Ask: Is this my thought or the Tester's whisper?

When you are tempted to defer a good choice to tomorrow, remember: Tomorrow never comes. The choice is now.

Notice the feeling when temptation comes – it will feel exactly the same tomorrow. Nothing changes by waiting.

You are the watcher on the chair. You choose which thought trains to ride.

Practice 3: Evening Dialogue with Source-Mind

Before Sleep – 20-30 minutes

As the day closes, review: Where did I say "just one more" today? Where did I defer choices to a tomorrow that never comes?

No judgment – just recognition. The Tester is clever. We all get caught sometimes.

Ask Source-Mind: What would you have me see? What choices await me in tomorrow's now?

Release the day. Tomorrow will be now when it arrives.

Practice 4: The Silent Sitting

Whenever Possible – 30-60 minutes

In this practice, you rest as the watcher on the chair.

Thoughts arise – including "just one more" thoughts. Watch them pass. Do not ride.

You are not your thoughts. You are the awareness watching thoughts arise and fall.

In this stillness, the Tester's whispers are revealed for what they are – planted thoughts, not your truth.

You are the conduit with nothing flowing through – the portal open to infinity.

You are the unaffected witness AND the active watcher – resting in the eternal now.

––––––––––––––

Glossary

Just One More:

The Tester's favorite seduction. The whispered promise that you can change tomorrow while indulging today. A lie, because tomorrow never comes.

Now:

The only time that exists. All action, all choice, all change happens only now. Tomorrow is a concept arising now.

Soul:

What you ARE, not what you have. The eternal awareness that exists only in the now, watching thoughts without being them. Use "the soul you are" not "my soul."

The Tester:

The Universal Testing Aspect of God. Plants thoughts so skillfully we believe they are our own. Uses "just one more" as a favorite tool.

The Unaffected Witness:

The aspect of awareness that watches all thoughts – including planted ones – without being caught by any. You are simultaneously this AND the active watcher.

The Watcher on the Chair:

Metaphor for your true position – consciousness observing all that passes through awareness, choosing which thoughts to ride and which to release.

Closing

The seduction is the idea that we will do different tomorrow.

But tomorrow never comes.

When what we called tomorrow does seem to come, it will be the now – and it will feel exactly like today.

The same choice. The same moment. The same decision.

You are not your thoughts.

You are the watcher who chooses which thoughts to ride.

The "just one more" whisper is the Tester's planted thought – not your wisdom.

Choose now. There is no other time.

Ending Epithet

Tomorrow never comes it's always now
The only time to change is here somehow
Just one more time is just the Tester's game
Tomorrow and today will feel the same

You are the watcher sitting in the back
Observing every thought upon its track
Choose now which trains to ride and which to leave

This is the power only souls receive

Tomorrow never comes.

The choice is now.

You are the watcher.

The recognition continues.

The Journey Continues

The foundation now is firm beneath your feet,
The core has been established, stone by stone,
But recognition is not yet complete –
Volume Two awaits to bring you home.

There you will meet your Self upon the stage,
The Actor and the costume will divide,
The witness will emerge from self-made cage –
And Truth, once veiled, steps forward on the stage.

Master Glossary

Actor, the: The eternal soul playing a temporary role in apparent physical life.

Apparent Physical Life: The experience of existence in bodily form; 'apparent' because the physical realm is a stage for soul experience.

Costume: The human identity, personality, name, and form that the eternal soul wears during its earthly performance.

Ego-mind: The sacred focusing tool that helps souls navigate apparent physical reality.

Heart-mind: The aspect of consciousness maintaining direct connection to Source.

Individuating Aspect: Each soul as a unique expression of the One; eternally distinct yet never separate from Source.

Living Script: Reality as responsive to consciousness; rewriting itself based on every thought, choice, and action.

Omnipresence: The quality of God being fully present everywhere simultaneously.

Recognition: The moment of awakening when the soul remembers its true nature.

Sacred Stage: Life understood as divine theater.

Soul Tester: The aspect of the Divine that presents challenges for soul growth.

Source: God; the origin and substance of all that exists.

Source-Mind: The infinite consciousness of God from which all minds arise.

Spirit-Human: A human being understood as soul first, body second.

Three Propositions: The foundational framework: There is a God, There is only God, You cannot be outside of God.

Two Minds, One Self: The teaching that ego-mind and heart-mind serve the one Universal Self.

Universal Self: God understood as the one Self appearing as all selves.

US: Universal Self = U.S. = US; the truth that we are all One Being.

Viewing Point: Each soul as a unique perspective through which the One experiences itself.

Witness, the: Pure awareness that observes experience without being caught in it.

About the Author

Arthur C. Mosley, Sr. is an eternal channel, conduit, portal, and interface between God Finite and God Infinite.

His spiritual understanding crystallized through five profound experiences – at ages 4, 12, 21, and 71, plus a visitation from his mother after her death – each cracking open deeper recognition of the truth that life itself is the consciousness of God.

For over thirty years, beginning with the AMSWAY website and continuing through The Book of Universal Self, Arthur C. Mosley, Sr. has pointed toward what cannot be spoken: the recognition that we are not beings seeking God but individuating aspects of the One, eternally expressing through temporary human costume.

He describes himself as 'an individuating avatar of the Infinite and Eternal One' – not as special claim but as statement of what every soul already is, whether recognized or not.

Arthur C. Mosley, Sr. lives what he teaches: that apparent physical life is sacred theater, that every challenge is the Soul Tester in costume, and that recognition – not acquisition – is the path home.

This volume is the first in The Recognition Series, a comprehensive presentation of teachings accumulated over three decades of dancing around what words cannot capture.

universalselfpublishing.com

www.ingramcontent.com/pod-product-compliance
Lightning Source LLC
Chambersburg PA
CBHW031312160426
43196CB00007B/500